THE POLYPOTENT MENTAL PROCESSOR

A NEW APPROACH TO THE MIND-BODY PROBLEM

GANESH BHARATE

To my Parents

Shrimati. Urmila Bharate

and

Shriman. Harishchandra Bharate

Contents

Preface

The mind is considered as mysterious because it is not given in any sense perception. Psychologists try to understand the mind through experiments in psychophysics through various measurements on sensory and cognitive capabilities. To establish a relationship between the mind-body is even more vexed as the body is given to us in sense perception and the mind is not. The mind is considered as higher level as it depends on the neural correlates. The instantiation of these neural correlates is identified with the conscious psychological processes. A causal relationship of how the higher-level exerts an influence over the lower-level, to alter the lower-level is referred to as Downward Causation. A thorough examination of Downward Causation is essential for understanding related phenomena in philosophy of mind, such as the nature of mental causation, emergence and self-organization. Philosophers belong to two camps when it comes to making a judgment over the concept of Downward Causation (henceforth DC). Firstly, those who accept DC are non-reductive physicalist, while those who oppose it are called reductive physicalist. Both reductionists and non-reductionists advocate a level hierarchy, starting with physics and progressing chronologically through chemistry, biology, psychology, and sociology on top of the Physical.

In the first chapter we state what are the specific questions that our book sets forth to answer. The first question is termed as correlational dualism. The view of supervenient epiphenomenalism based on mind-brain correlational studies leaves the mind "hanging" outside the causal nexus of the physical. Parallelism, on the other hand, states that mind-body processes are perfectly coordinated given Leibniz's pre-established harmony analysis. Taking these two statements to their logical conclusion, the problem statement is posed that epiphenomenalism is in the same boat as parallelism. This is the central issue addressed by the book, and it is termed the 'problem of correlational dualism.'.

If the mental states or higher-level phenomena depend on the lower-level physical states, the concept of downward causation faces the problem of self-causation. Self-causation in this sense becomes absurd because the higher-level which is dependent on ontological existence on the lower-level is causally influencing that very lower-level which makes the existence of the higher-level possible. What role does multiple realizability pay in the context of DC when the higher levels emerge and acquire causal powers? What are the appropriate conditions to be imposed while coherently formulating DC? On a similar note, we can say in principle that multiple mental states (mentation) can be instantiated by the same physical substrate, which the author refers to as the concept of 'polymentation' the inverse of multiple realizability.

In the second chapter we very ask whether DC is a misunderstanding or a legitimate concept. Two concerns are raised against DC in the Philosophical literature viz. that DC does not have consensus over what does it mean by causation and the second one is about what is relata in DC is not clear. By analyzing the existing literature, we state that DC is a legitimate concept and there is a consensus developing that, revival of Aristotelian fourfold causation is important in order to understand DC. The relata in DC is construed as generic events, powers or tropes as against the standard event ontology of causation. Rather than these two problems we raise a question that the dependency relation of supervenience in DC is a bigger threat that the problems of consensus on causation or relata of causation.

In the third chapter, we discuss three forms of reductionism viz. constructivist, intertheoretical and mereological. We then see what implications the reductionist approach has in the Philosophy of mind. The reductionist approach culminates in the identity theory of brain-mind specifically into, 'is of strict identity'. With this position in the back of our minds, we pose five problems to the identity theory. The first problem is from biology well known as the problem of the gut-brain axis, phantom limbs and brainless creatures which require something more than the brain in its explanation. The second problem is in the domain of psychology known as the placebo effect which has a disruptive pathway induced by beliefs as against the neural pathway. The third problem arises in the legal domain termed as 'habeas cerebrum' which means that if the brain processes are causally responsible for all behaviour, then the part causally accountable alone should be the part which should not be unnecessarily detained. The question regarding the person's body does not arise as only the brain processes are culpable. The fourth problem is that of necessary and sufficient conditions, a logical problem. The brain states are sufficient but not necessary as given by the concept of multiple realizability. The mental phenomena can be actualized in silicon-based or in some other suitable substratum as well. The fifth problem is stated as the hard problem of reduction where the problem of reducing Stenberg's theory of love to the molecule of love 'oxytocin' is raised. Finally, we discuss the epistemic virtue viz. principle of charity and how should we interpret the causal efficacy of the mental states is left open.

The fourth chapter on framework elaborates on three broad backgrounds viz. framework one is the relation of inherence as against the dependency relation of supervenience. The second framework is that of robust reductionism as against eliminative reductionism. The third is the framework of Basic Formal Ontology to represent the mind/self within the larger picture of existing entities. The fifth chapter poses the question of self-causation which complicates the concept of downward causation. This problem is created due to the acceptance of transitivity in causation that the cause should always be temporally before the effect. Later we discuss enabling and disabling constraints in self-organizing systems, which act at the same temporal instant and are causal. This can aid in the resolution of the self-causation problem.

The sixth chapter expands on our claim that causal powers are critical in making DC a coherent concept. We first state the mental functioning ontology (MFO) which is similar to the identity theory.

The MFO does not consider the distinction between specifically dependent continuants and generically dependent continuants. We use this classificatory concept of generically dependent continuant to characterize the nature of the mind. The mind is construed as an information-content entity, generically dependent upon the person. The mind inheres in the person, not in the brain. We claim that the mind is partially autonomous and has causal powers if we analyse function, unity, property and information (FUPI). Finally, we provide a pragmatic justification for the autonomy of psychological explanation based on the fact that psychotherapy works. Rather than going on the traditional path and asking whether there are psychological laws or not to claim autonomy, we choose a pragmatic path. In the last chapter, we conclude our book and state what could be the limitations and possible future work which could be done. The image of the peacock on the title page is a symbolism for the concept of mind engendered through the book. I invite all the readers on this inquisitive path to understand the nature of mind.

Acknowledgements

I would like to thank and acknowledge my thesis supervisor Dr. A. V. Ravishankar Sarma as he gave me an opportunity to engage in this quest. The book would not have been possible without his time-to-time advice and guidance. Special thanks to his way of doing research work by explicitly giving a problem statement at the very outset so that the writing gets a clear direction.

Acknowledgement is a lesser word to show my indebtedness to my parents who supported me in my journey. Without my parent's support, I would not have explored and come to know in the first place my love for Philosophy. PhD is not only an intellectual journey, but it tests the person's integrity, emotional maturity and one's stress-bearing capacity. So, I would like to give my acknowledgements to the people in my life who loved me. The images on the front page are compiled from creative commons freely available to download or use.

CHAPTER ONE

The Mind does not Matter

I keep six honest serving-men
They taught me all I knew
Their names are What and Why and When
And How and Where and Who
........Rudyard Kipling (1902)

1.1 Introduction

The concept of Downward Causation (DC) is understood as a relation of the causal influence of the mental states on the physical states in the Philosophy of mind. If we generalize this concept then what we get is, that any of the higher-levels exerting a causal influence over the lower-level is called downward causation. The causal influence of lower-levels in the sense of material cause; constituting, and influencing the higher-level is acknowledged by and is coherent within a physicalist framework. The physicalist thesis is that if at all there is a causal influence, it is a physical influence i.e. the physical is causally closed, called the principle of causal closure. If we apply this principle, all non-physical levels corresponding to sciences other than physics, also called special sciences (Fodor 2013) do not have any causal role to play. The special sciences are thereby excluded from causal efficacy, given causal reduction to the micro-level, to whatever is the bottom-most physical level.

We debate causal reduction to micro physical level and causal exclusion within this book. The book presupposes the existing literature on downward causation viz. rejecting microphysicalism (Mumford and Anjum 2017) and accepting a causal slack (Ellis 2009) in physical, making the principle of causal closure unacceptable. This paves the way toward the second question of whether causal exclusion holds when we reject the principle of causal closure of the microphysical. This is a simple way in which we can depict the problem that upward causation from physical to other levels is acceptable but downward causation i.e. influence of the higher-level on the lower-level is debatable.

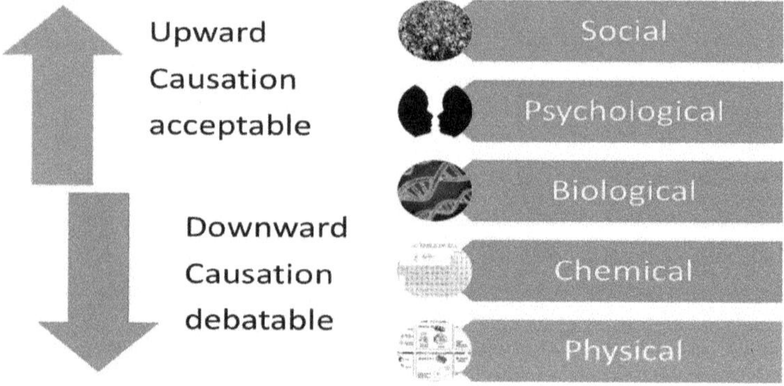

Figure 1 Reductionist view regarding upward and downward causation

In the above figure, we can observe that the special sciences are marked in red colour as they do not have causal efficacy and if at all they have causal efficacy would entail correspondingly to the concept of downward causation. Whereas the entities in the physical marked in green colour makeup causally efficacious realm and hence a respected citizen of our physicalist ontology. This physicalist ontology is causally closed, and entities causally interact only within this ontology.

The principle of causal closure rests on the epistemic virtue of Ockham's razor wherein we reduce the entities to a minimum which populate our ontology with only causal explanatory purposes. This causal closure and causal exclusion are backed by the methodology of apriori reduction developed from the razor used in ontology. Supervenience is a relation where the mental states or higher-level states are co-instantiated by the fundamental lower-level.

> I hold, as an a priori principle, that every contingent truth must be made true, somehow, by the pattern of instantiation of fundamental properties and relations. The whole truth about the world, including the mental part of the world, supervenes on this pattern. If two possible worlds were exactly isomorphic in their patterns of coinstantiation of fundamental properties and relations, they would thereby be exactly alike simpliciter. (Lewis 1999)

This position of apriori reductionism which leads to the position of physicalism is criticized in the famous Hempel's dilemma (Stoljar 2010). The first horn of the dilemma states that physicalism as a position is problematic because physics as a science is incomplete in its current situation given science is an ongoing process. The second horn of the dilemma states that if we bank upon future physics which will reduce the mind to a lower-level we face the fallacy of resting our case on the future which is now unknown. Given this background, we pose certain problems which we would like to address in this book.

According to causal pluralism (Godfrey-Smith 2009), causation is fundamentally a cluster concept, and holding only one notion of causation will lead to problems of coherence elsewhere. The current dissertation is concerned with the role of causal pluralism in comprehending the phenomenon of downward causation. For example, if we accept the probability theory of causation it can capture the chanciness very nicely, but it cannot explain why such a relation holds. In the hierarchy of structure, as broadly defined by the various domains of sciences, both upward and downward causation occur. Bottom-up causation corresponds to how physicists think, in which lower-level processes cause higher-level phenomena. In downward causation cases, the higher-level gains autonomy due to novel properties and influences the lower-level. In this dissertation, we investigate the influence of higher-levels on lower-levels using causal powers. In contrast to the Humean events ontology of causation, causal powers ontology is an alternative ontology of causation. We state the pragmatically consistent necessary and sufficient conditions for downward causation to occur in the conclusion of the book. Many philosophers maintained that downward causation is a misnomer and a fictitious concept, thus beyond the scope of reductionists. We argue against this viewpoint and propose a theory of causal powers that allows us to talk rationally and pragmatically about downward causation. The dissertation aims to provide answers to the following specific questions:

1.2 Problem statement

Now we define the specific problems that concern the author. Although there are many problems that downward causation faces to be established as a coherent concept, we narrow down the scope of the book to answer these prominent questions. Firstly, what is the consequence of accepting supervenience as a dependency relation between the higher and lower-level, and how is the mind co-instantiated by the lower-level processes? The second problem arises from accepting transitivity in upward causation based on supervenience leading to the problem of self-causation. Third, we talk about the conditions for the possibility of DC mainly multiple realizability and its converse polymentation.

- The view of supervenient epiphenomenalism based on mind-brain correlational studies leaves the mind "hanging" outside the causal nexus of the physical. Parallelism, on the other hand, states that mind-body processes are perfectly coordinated given

Leibniz's pre-established harmony analysis. Taking these two statements to their logical conclusion, the problem statement is posed that epiphenomenalism faces the same plight as parallelism. This is the central issue addressed by the book, and it is termed the 'problem of correlational dualism.'.

- If the mental states or higher-level phenomena depend on the lower-level physical states, the concept of downward causation faces the problem of self-causation. Self-causation in this sense becomes absurd because the higher-level which is dependent on ontological existence on the lower-level is causally influencing that very lower-level which makes the existence of the higher-level possible.

- How does the key feature of DC, multiple realizability, act in the context of causal powers? What are the appropriate conditions to be imposed while coherently formulating DC? On a similar note, we can say in principle that multiple mental states (mentation) can be instantiated by the same physical substrate, which the author refers to as the concept of 'polymentation' the converse of multiple realizability.

Can we attribute the process of higher-level influencing lower within a causal powers view of causation? If this is the case, what role do causal powers play in downward causation? We represent the mind in Basic Formal Ontology and analyse the concepts of function, unity, property and information (FUPI) in the last chapter. We claim that this analysis leads to a coherent conception of downward causation where the mind is partially autonomous and has apomatic powers.

Is correlation causal?

The first problem which we have coined correlational dualism arises due to the acceptance of supervenience as a dependency relation that requires us to assess what is correlation. Correlation is often misunderstood as causation. So, we first need a basic understanding of correlation which we believe will help in further understanding our work.

Let us begin by stating what is correlation. The term correlation refers to the measurement of variables that are statistically related linearly. It is primarily used to depict relationships without passing judgement on the cause-effect relationship between them. The two most important terms in determining statistical correlation are the correlation coefficient (r) and statistical significance (p-value). The correlational coefficient 'r' can range from -1 to + 1. In the absence of an effect, the statistical significance p-value is an indicator of the likelihood of finding data that we want to observe. The p-value ranges from 0 to 1, with 0 representing no chance or probability and 1 representing certainty of the null hypothesis. As a result, the lower the p-value, the weaker the null hypothesis and the stronger the alternative hypothesis. As a result, statistical significance determines whether the correlation is due to chance or not.

The question regarding whether the phrase 'statistically significant' or the concept of p-value should be discontinued from usage (Mayo and Hand 2022) is an ongoing controversy. For our purposes, these questions are significant concerning correlation. How are brain states correlated to mental states? What verification is required for determining a state a brain state or a mental state? How are correlational studies performed and what are the machines used to measure such a relation?

Brain states are validated using EEG (Electro Encephalogram) or fMRI (functional Magnetic Resonance Imaging), whereas the mental states are validated through a subjective report or behavioural testing. It is a tall claim to establish a causal relationship from correlation when mental states are of a different 'kind' than brain states. The main reason for this is the debate over whether fMRI data is about blood flow in the region of interest rather than neural dynamics correlated with subjective reports of psychological states. As a result, the inferential process is not directly dependent on neural dynamics, but blood flow is only an indicator of the underlying neural processes (Vul et.al. 2009).

The brain activity is directly measured in the case of EEG but it is unclear whether the electrical-magnetic stimulus is from the surface or the deep brain (Kilner 2013). Correlations in social neuro-scientific studies may also be due to noise, with reports of these relationships being exaggerated. Other studies in the field argue that these correlations are not voodoo, but rather genuine correlations with a minor bias (Lieberman and Cunningham 2009). The nature of empirical claims based on direct observation is fraught with induction problems. Thus, correlations based on indirect indicators of neural activity are at best debatable in terms of their validity. Blood flow in the brain region is an indirect inferential base for actual neural activity to conclude in mind-brain identity. Blood flow is correlated with the areas activated in the brain.

To advance the next argument against such correlational studies we need to first understand the concept of causation by absence. Take a simple example, let us assume someone asks why you are late today for the class, and the student replies, that the bus to college did not arrive. So, the cause of someone being late to college is the absence of the bus. If we bring in the concept of causation by absence, that even parts where activity is not seen might have some causal role to play, then the correlation studies might require more robust criteria for assigning correlation. So, we need markers to assign apart from the parts in the brain that glow also what might not be shown in the images but could be causally relevant.

To summarize, the strong mind-brain identity relation will face a problem similar to Hempel's dilemma in that the current scientific study does not state an identity between the brain and mind, and if we rely on future scientific studies, we will be resting on unknown ground. Thus, the 'correlational dualism' problem confronts the strong identity theory. If the mind is identical to brain states and not dependent on it holding a supervenience relation, the entire supervenience discussion collapses. If the supervenience relation is correct in understanding the mind-brain relationship, then we are correlating mind with mind or brain states with brain states, because mind and brain are identical. As a result, we require an alternative to supervenience and an alternative to strict identity.

After demonstrating the dangers of such positions, we present our account of identity and dependency relationships, demonstrating how mental qua mental can have causal powers of its own.

1.3 Structure of the book

In the first chapter, we have introduced which problems are set forth that the book will dwell upon. The three problems are as follows. The first problem is coined as 'correlational dualism' which comes forth due to the acceptance of supervenience as a dependency relation. Supervenience excludes granting any causal powers to the mind. To counter this problem, we give an alternate dependency relation of inherence.

The second problem is about self-causation as in how it is possible that the higher-level which relies upon the lower-level for its continuance, causally influence the lower-level. It is nonsensical to think that self-causation is possible. To this, we have replied in the fifth chapter that if causation is construed as constraints, then the absurdity of self-causation can be overcome.

The third question is how does the mind acquire causal powers and under what conditions does downward causation take place without violating our scientific understanding of the world? We have answered this question in the sixth chapter where we analyse function, unity, property and information (FUPI), in virtue of these mind accrues causal powers.

In the second chapter two concerns are raised which makes downward causation a misnomer. The first concern is that; it is unclear as to what is causal relata in DC. The second concern is that there is no consensus as to what causation in DC is. We state from the existing literature that generic events, powers and tropes are considered as relata in DC. While regarding causation there is a growing consensus that Aristotelian fourfold causation should be invoked to make DC a viable concept. We raise a concern regarding the dependency relation between higher and lower-levels which is rather a bigger problem for DC than the concerns of relata and causation. An alternative dependency relation is given in the fourth chapter on the framework named relational inherence.

In the third chapter, we witness two opposing viewpoints have been developed in the literature. One such viewpoint is reductionism, which is influenced by the empiricist tradition that eliminates mental causation. The other is that of Emergentists accepting mental causation in a non-reductive physicalist framework. According to reductionist philosophers (Carnap 1963, Oppenhiem and Putnam 1958, Nagel 1935), all causal powers reside at the lower-level, and special sciences (sciences other than physics) and especially the mind are epiphenomenal. So, first and foremost, one must comprehend the reductionist position. For comprehending the reductionist position, we review various reductionisms classified as constructivist, intertheoretical, or mereological.

Finally, what impact does reductionism have on philosophical debates about identity reduction? The other view within the non-reductive physicalist framework (Fodor 2013, Campbell 1974, Sperry 1980, Morgan 1925, Alexander 1920), Emergentists claim that the special sciences and the mind possess irreducible causal powers, and these can be explained within a non-reductive physicalism framework. DC renders these opposing positions of reductionism and emergentism as mutually consistent and co-existing. It is the position of functionalists that multiple realizability plays an important role. Putnam (Putnam 1967, Fodor 2013) advanced the multiple realizability argument, which contradicts the reductive strict identity of mind-brain. The principle of causal closure can be weakened by rejecting micro-physicalism that all causality drains to the lowest physical level and by accepting a causal porosity/slack at the lowest physical level.

Recently, Mumford and Anjum (2017) argued against reductionists, by first weakening the principle of causal closure and then using the causal dispositional-transformative account to challenge micro-physicalism. We conclude that DC is a viable concept within methodological reductionism that merits further investigation within a conducive framework. Reductionists have their rationale and Emergentists have their rationale which we discuss at the end of the third chapter as the battle of epistemic virtues on which each of them rests i.e. Ockham's razor and the principle of charity respectively.

Is there a way out of this impasse? The Reductionists and the Emergentists both have valid arguments for reducing the higher-levels to lower for unification and claiming higher-levels are autonomous for causal-explanatory purposes. The claims of the Reductionist and Emergentist camps are discussed in the third chapter, proceeding with methodological reductionism (Wimsatt 2006), leading to a position of non-eliminative realism. The issues of supervenience, grounding, and inherence are discussed as dependency relations. Given these issues with dependency relationships, the framework chapter elaborates on the alternative mind-body dependency termed, relational inherence. The fourth chapter of the framework discusses the relation of inherence as best suited to discussing DC. Given the various backgrounds that comprise the framework, the reductionists' assumptions are revealed.

The third framework of the book is Basic Formal Ontology (BFO). All existing phenomena, according to BFO, are divided into two categories: occurrents and continuants. Occurents are ongoing processes that occur, whereas continuants are named because they continue to exist and exhibit some form of stability. Because the special sciences and mind exist even though their internal constituents change, they can be classified as continuants with respect to the underlying occurrent lower-level processes. It is argued that only occurents have causal powers because they are fundamental (Simons 2013).

In the sixth chapter, we examine the ontological status of the mind in light of the earlier analysis of identity theory concerning Basic Formal Ontology (BFO). The dissertation argues for continuants' causal powers through an examination of property, unity, context, and function. Continuants are classified into two types: independent continuants, and dependent continuants. Again, dependent continuants are classified further into specifically dependent continuants and generically dependent continuants. Ignoring the distinction between specifically dependent and generically dependent continuants has resulted in unintended consequences such as rejecting the causal influence of mind and special sciences. Given their causal-explanatory power, it is concluded that special sciences and the mind are inhering (Bradley 2017) in the physical rather than supervene on it. We corroborate this inherence with the understanding that powers inhere and are directed because of intentionality, the position regarding causal relation taken by Psillos (2021).

> ...it takes powers and their manifestations (or exercises) not to be reducible to the instantiations of non-power properties or to event-causal sequences. According to this robustly realistic view about powers, powers are properties which are essentially 'directed at' certain changes. (Mayr 2017)

Causal powers play an important role in avoiding the problems created by events ontology of causation. The causal reducibility of mind to brain states due to supervenience is questioned given problems with type identity because of multiple realizability and problems with token identity because of polymentation Now if the Eleatic principle is true, it is argued that when special sciences or the mind has causal explanatory value then one is not populating the ontology with supernatural entities, but such entities have a respectable position in our ontology.

While avoiding one problem of Cartesian interactionism, Occam's razor used in reductionism ends up with another problem of parallelism because it reduces the higher-level and characterizes the higher-level as epiphenomenal. The central claim of the book is that, while the special sciences and mind are dependent on lower-level physical states through inherence, they gain partial autonomy as analysed by the concepts of property, unity, function, and information (FUPI). This characteristic of dependence and autonomy is known as "Apophenomena," which is opposed to the concept of epiphenomena.

There are plenty of other problems and issues, but we do not go into these issues viz. subjectivity, qualia, personhood, self, consciousness etc. allied to the problems of DC. We only stick to the problems about causal aspects of the mind or in general to the higher-levels. In the concluding chapter, we show what is the significance that our study has given to the existing literature. Then we show what is the limitation of our work. In which scenarios the claim will be nullified? Given the limitation of what future work can be engaged in? With this, we conclude our book.

CHAPTER TWO

Is Downward Causation a Misnomer?

"...if it isn't literally true that my wanting is causally responsible for my reaching, and my itching is causally responsible for my scratching, and my believing is causally responsible for my saying...if none of that is literally true, then practically everything I believe about anything is false and it's the end of the world."

Jerry Fodor (1998)

It has been argued that Downward Causation in general is a misnomer (Hulswit 2005) due to the ambiguity of the relata and meaning of causation in Downward Causation. To view it as a misnomer is primarily a matter of the meaning that the concept implies. If only one criterion for causation, such as production making is true, even simple cases such as billiard ball motion may not be explained, which are otherwise well explained by regularity and energy transfer accounts of causation. Does causal explanation necessitate a specific account of causation in specific domains or cases? Is the account of reductive and non-reductive physicalism contradictory, or does each have its explanatory value within the larger framework of Physicalism? The third issue is raised regarding level dependency, which undermines the concept of downward causation. So, how is the concept of Downward Causation problematic, and how do philosophers who argue for it defend it? Given arguments on both sides, the question of whether Downward Causation is a viable concept, or a misnomer is an intriguing one.

E.g. if we take a position like Descartes that the mind is a substance which does not have an extension in space then how will the mind interact with something which is in space? But if we take a position like Aristotle's substance which is the substratum of properties and about which something is predicated then we do not have a problem of interactionism created by the very definition of substance. We are of the view that within the existing literature we have answers for these two concerns. The answer to the question regarding relata can be seen as generic events, tropes and powers. While the answer to the question regarding consensus on causation in DC can be seen as a revival of Aristotelian fourfold causation. A graver question than these two is rather stating what dependency relation makes DC not a misnomer as supervenience precludes DC.

In our everyday discourse, we discuss how we are motivated to engage in certain behaviour, with the reasons being our beliefs, desires, background knowledge, and so on. Our beliefs, desires, and volitions are the reasons for our behaviour, according to our linguistic usage. Mental desires and beliefs are at a higher mental level, motivating the individual to act. Thus, we observe that there is certainly influence from social to individual and mental to behavioural; however, when we are asked where society is independent of individuals or where the mind is independent of biological processes, there is nothing obvious to show.

So, while we intuitively believe that top-down influences are commonplace, we have no answers to the existential status of any higher-level apart from its constituents at the lower-level in a more reflective mode. The integrated whole is said to be at a higher-level than the constituent parts, and the existence of a higher is dependent on the existence of a lower. Individuals are seen as parts of a larger whole in this context. In the second case, neurons are parts and neural firing patterns are the whole, and we see that there is influence from the whole to its parts as well as the dependency of the higher-level on the lower-level. How can the higher-level, which is dependent on the lower-level because the lower-level is constitutive, influence the lower-level causally? We'll start by looking at how DC is defined in the literature.

2.1 What is Downward Causation?

Downward Causation is a term used to grasp the idea that there is a causal influence of the higher-level on the lower-level. We intuitively think of reality as having a hierarchical structure, similar to the domains of empirical sciences such as physics, chemistry, biology, psychology, and sociology. Physics is the most fundamental of the empirical sciences, and it is at the bottom of the hierarchy, while the latter is formed by the increasing order of complexity in the physical domain.

Thus, the fundamental particles of physics are elements and molecules, which are studied by chemistry. Biological entities are made up of atoms and molecules. Biological entities endowed with sentience and consciousness form colonies and societies. The most important reason for viewing ontological reality as a level hierarchy is that the higher-level is made up of the lower-level. Both reductionists and Emergentists accept a hierarchy of levels which depicts reality. Thus, there is a constitutive relationship between the objects of inquiry of one empirical science and those constituted by the base science's more fundamental building blocks. However, not all constitutive relations form a higher and lower-level. An earthen pot, for example, is made of clay, but no one would say that the pot is at a higher-level and the clay is at a lower-level.

A level is also defined by a complex of internal relations among the parts and external relations of the whole to its environment. These levels are said to be emergent, and they are not mysterious because they correspond to empirical sciences. Although many more intermediate levels can be added to each pair of levels, for general purposes, any minimum number greater than or equal to two suffices. The interlevel relationship is not the same throughout the hierarchy.

The inter-level relations are non-homomorphic in the sense that the emergence of the biological from the physical level in the sense that the emergence of the biological from the physical level does not have the same complex on the inter-level relations of dependence as the emergence of the social and psychic levels from the biological one (Andersen 2000)

Homo means same and morph means form, in the case of the emergence of the biological realm from the physical realm the above quote suggests that the form is not the same at each level. Even though biological, psychological, and social levels are dependent and constituted by the physical the complexity at each level is different. Hence the interlevel relation between say physical-psychological or physical-social is not the same.

There are various criteria on which the idea of levels is justified. We have scale (McGivern 2013), constitution, mechanistic, correspondence with a scientific domain, level as a category of understanding, heuristic, and universe of discourse (Brooks 2017). The levels of the hierarchy shown below, as we can observe have a correspondence with the fields of sciences and a bifurcation can be seen after the very first level of physics viz. organic and physical chemistry. The further hierarchy in the living matter above chemistry is biochemistry whereas above physical chemistry is material sciences. Such a hierarchy of levels can be seen both in inanimate matter and living matter. We can observe below that levels can be depicted taking into consideration inanimate and animate matter. Levels of hierarchy correspond with the domains of scientific enquiry. A levels hierarchy is a minimal requirement for the possibility of downward causation. If one does not accept levels, then there is no question about upward or downward causation.

Hierarchy of levels given by Ellis;

Level	Inanimate matter	Living Matter
Level 8	Cosmology	Sociology
Level 7	Astronomy	Psychology
Level 6	Space science	Physiology
Level 5	Geology	Cell Biology
Level 4	Materials science	Biochemistry
Level 3	Physical chemistry	Chemistry
Level 2	Atomic physics	Atomic physics
Level 1	Fundamental theory	Fundamental theory

Table 1 The basic hierarchy of inanimate matter and for life, with minor changes from the original table pg.88 (Ellis 2016)

The remaining chapter is structured as follows. The second section provides a classification and further elaboration of the concept of DC. The third section investigates the first objection that the relata of DC are not clear. The fourth section delves into DC's second objection to a consensus regarding 'causation' in DC. The fifth section concludes and summarizes the debate and discussion.

Examples from the social domain are used to simplify understanding of the influence of higher-levels on the lower. Individual intentions, for example, are manipulated through advertisements and social media influence. Another example would be a social influence on an individual's behaviour, such as how an individual behaves differently in front of a) parents, b) friends, c) while anonymous, and d) in a mob. The social impact theory (Latané 1981) gives an equation $I = f (SIN)$ gives the social influence (I) over an individual, where social impact (I) is supposed to be a function of strength (S), immediacy (I), and number (N). To some extent, the individual's behaviour is influenced by the social context in which they find themselves. As a result, society as a whole influence the individual as a part of it. The whole is at a higher-level, whereas the parts are at a lower-level. This influence must be scrutinized under which understanding of causation can be considered causal. DC is defined as follows in the Encyclopaedia of Neuroscience.

Downward Causation exists if the system parts are to some degree constrained by the whole, which is the converse of the principle that the microstructure of a system determines the system properties and dispositions. (Dronkers and Baldo 2009)

One can say that there is downward causation in a system if the parts of a system are coerced or constrained to some degree. This is the opposite of how we understand that the lower-level mechanisms and properties determine or influence how the higher-level behaves.

In our everyday discourse, we discuss how we are motivated to engage in certain behaviour, with the reasons being our beliefs, desires, background knowledge, and so on. Our beliefs, desires, and volitions are the reasons for our behaviour, according to our linguistic usage. Mental desires and beliefs are at a higher mental level, motivating the individual to act. Thus, we observe that there is certainly influence from social to individual and mental to behavioural; however, when we are asked where society is independent of individuals or where the mind is independent of biological processes, there is nothing obvious to show. So, while we intuitively believe that top-down influences are commonplace, we have no answers to the existential status of any higher-level apart from its constituents at the lower-level in a more reflective mode. The integrated whole is said to be at a higher-level than the constituent parts, and the existence of a higher is dependent on the existence of a lower. Individuals are seen as parts of a larger whole in this context. In the second case, neurons are parts and neural firing patterns are the whole, and we see that there is influence from the whole to its parts as well as the dependency of the higher-level on the lower-level. How can the higher-level, which is dependent on the lower-level because the lower-level is constitutive, influence the lower-level causally? We'll start by looking at how DC is defined in the literature.

2.2 Classification based on the strength

The first attempt at the classification of DC was done by (Andersen 2000). The classification is based on four hypotheses and depends on conditions as to which assumptions are fulfilled to categorize the type of DC. The four hypotheses are, 1a) Constitutive reductionism – the lower-level entities constitute the higher-level, the higher-level is not reducible but does not add any substance to the lower-level. 1b) Constitutive irreductionism – even though materially the higher-level is constituted of lower-level entities, the higher-level is supposed to constitute its substance. 2a) Formal realism of levels – the structure, organization or form exists objectively and cannot be reduced to the lower-level entities. 2b) Substantial realism of levels – the structure or the form is necessary but not sufficient for the higher-level and there is an ontological change in the substance through emergence. Combining these four definitions DC is classified into strong, medium and weak based on their strength. We will now go over these topics in greater depth. This classification is important as it marks the starting point from where the issue of DC becomes contested.

2.2.1 Strong Downward Causation

In the strong type of DC, an entity or process can affect or change the entities or processes at a lower-level. For strong DC to occur, hypotheses 1b) constitutive irreductionism and 2b) substantial realism must be satisfied. For example, the cell transforms non-living molecules into specifically biologically living molecules. If we consider the example, it is unclear how the cell differs substantially from the biomolecules that comprise it. How are cells a different substance than biomolecules?

It is claimed that this view is incorrect because it leads to substance dualism in the manner of Descartes, and no contemporary philosopher holds this viewpoint. As a result, this classification is historically significant for categorizing various perspectives on DC. However, as we can see, Cartesian dualism is not hierarchical, and both substances are equal by definition of being a substance - that which exists independently in itself. As a result, I believe this classification does not serve as a historical classification account. Paoletti (2017), however, has argued in recent literature for the DSSC - Downward Substance Structural Causation model. Paoletti defines substance (2016) as an ontologically basic, primary subject of change, and typified by kinds. 'I,' according to Paoletti, is a substance. Aside from the viewpoint of disembodied subjects, in contemporary philosophy of mind, we do not see such a position claiming that the subject is completely independent, as brain damage studies (Parfit 2008) have shown that the mind is dependent on the brain. Substance in the Aristotelian sense of substratum and subject about which something is predicated can be coherently used as a definition of substance without falling into the trap of Cartesian dualism.

2.2.2 Medium Downward Causation

There is no direct causation in this form; the higher-level imposes a constraining feature on the lower-level. It argues for the conditions 1b) constitutive irreductionism combined with both, 2a) formal realism of levels and 2b) substantial realism of levels. For example, the already realized higher-level, such as the organism as a whole, moves tissues and so on without interfering with them. The higher-level is not significantly different in this case, and there is no efficient causation. The higher-level is constitutionally, organizationally, and concerning the constituents at the lower-level. Causation in this form of DC is a formal cause, where the higher-level structures constrain the lower-levels by imposing boundary conditions on them.

2.2.3 Weak Downward Causation

The higher-level entity attracts lower-level dynamics in this form of DC. It combines 1a) constitutive reductionism and 2a) level formal realism. This form is found in systems where attractor patterns and state space are common features, such as macrophysics, solid state physics, cosmology, and so on, rather than in transitions between large levels. WDC may only imply epistemic and explanatory roles, rather than any ontological causal relationship. The authors do not completely agree on all forms of DC, but they do agree on the formal cause (of the four Aristotelian causes). As higher-level entities (e.g., a cell) supervene on lower-order entities (e.g., molecules), formal causality on the higher-level supervenes on efficient causality on the lower-levels. The Supervenience relation is a relationship of dependence between higher and lower-levels. If there are two levels X and Y, there is no change in Y if there is no change in X, where Y at the higher-level is dependent on X at the lower-level. In this type of relationship, how can the higher-level acquire any causal powers? So, given the Supervenience relation, establishing the claim that formal causality of the higher-level supervenes on efficient causality of the lower-level necessitates more justification. A relation of Inherence (Aristotle 2014, Patterson 2017) is far superior to the relation of Supervenience, which was the dominant view of dependence in the philosophy of mind at the time.

Two views are formed while explaining the influence of the higher-level over the lower-level viz. reductive physicalism and non-reductive physicalism. Reductive physicalism rejects any possibility of higher-level having any causal influence on the lower-level because the higher-level supervenes on the lower-level or is reducible to the lower-level. On the other hand, non-reductive physicalism has a non-reducible aspect to the higher-level which bestows it with a capacity to causally influence the lower-level, a capacity which is stripped off by the reductionists.

Even though we have such a classification of DC in the literature as stated above the concept of DC is relegated to being a misnomer. The reason for calling the concept of DC a misnomer is twofold. Firstly, it is not clear as to what is the relata in DC and secondly, there is no consensus as to what constitutes causation in DC. We will try to understand these two problems and their answers of it within the existing literature.

2.3 First Objection- Relata in Downward Causation

The question of what is relata in DC is problematic (Hulswit 2005) because philosophers who argue for DC do not accept the standard formulation of causation (efficient), as we will see in the next section while analysing the second objection. Orilia and Paoletti (2017) classified DC relata into three categories: generic events, tropes, and powers (Orilia, Paoletti 2017). The majority of philosophers, including Hume (1896), Kim (1993), and Davidson (2002) argue that events are the causal relata. Any event requires an object x, which instantiates a property P and occurs at time-t; this is represented as [(x, t) P]. This requirement has resulted in various quandaries in DC, as there is no object independent of the lower-level parts, as there is no specific object and only a whole which occupies a hazy location, which cannot be shown as an object independent of its parts, and the nature of higher-level is both synchronic and diachronic cannot be stated as happening at specific time t1 or t2. If mental events are considered non-physical, the ontology of the event for DC must violate the physical causal closure principle. In this case, the generic mental event is the supervenient cause of the specific physical event, and thus the generic event is causal of that specific physical event, and thus DC is possible.

The supervenient state of mind is weakly causally related and not by the strong nomological notion of supervenience, according to the multiple realization thesis. This weaker version of supervenience results in weak causal closure, and thus generic events do not face Kim's problem of strong causal closure (Orilia and Paoletti 2017). According to Yablo (1992), in two competing causes, the proportional cause wins the race, certifying the mental cause over the neural cause, which was relegated epiphenomenal by the overdetermination argument. For example, one raises the arm to answer a question, cleans the ceiling, grabs a box from a shelf and hit someone. These four are generic instances of the specific instance of raising the arm. If one accepts Yablo's proportionality condition, then that generic event is the cause of raising the arm. With the acceptance of Yablo's test, one has to sacrifice the physical causal closure then generic events become candidates for strong downward causation. By weak supervenience, the generic mental event causes the specific physical realizer to be instantiated, and thus generic events can be viewed as downwardly causal.

Second, relata are regarded as tropes, which refer to specific non-shareable instances of properties. Some property instances characterize a trope as mental, while others characterize a trope as physical. An object is classified as mental (subjectivity, intentionality) or physical (fundamental forces, fundamental particles) based on a set of unified properties. A distinction is made between two objects based on certain characteristics. The Physical is a proper subset of the mental objects in general, and a physical realizer in particular. The mental and physical cannot be considered type identical due to multiple realizations. The question is whether being a mental unified trope or a physical unified trope causes the mental; where does the causal power reside? There is no causal role for the mental if no overdetermination is accepted within a reductive physicalism framework given causal closure.

If non-reductive physicalism is accepted based on token identity, then the causal role is played by the non-reductively physical mental, which is token identical to the physical realizer. Wilson (2011) uses the power-based subset strategy to argue that the mental causal power is a proper subset of the physical powers, that the mental is individualized, and that the mental realizer is token identical to the physical realizer. Because the physical realizer is performing causal work and the mental state is identical to the token realizer, one can be convinced to say that the mental state is performing causal work. For the scientific and causal explanatory process, any non-causal aspect of the mind is irrelevant. Wilson uses the terms quiddity and distinct property of mental states instead of individual tropes, so the property is taken to mean power, and powers are causal relata. So we can observe that specifics regarding causal relata are available in the existing literature on DC.

Once we introduce causal powers into the picture, we may well see causation in general as the exercise of causal powers by substances, i.e., entities endowed with causal powers ...we must say that a substance, by exercising a certain power, causes a certain event. This allows one to reduce, as Lowe puts it, event causation to substance causation. (Orilia and Paoletti 2017)

Thus, we can observe that in DC, a substance in the Aristotelian sense is regarded as causal relata, as the causation of an event is reduced to the causation by substance. However, it should be noted that the meaning of substance in this context differs from the Cartesian definition. According to Descartes (Slowik 2001), the substance is that which exists independently of itself, while according to Aristotle (Gill 1989), the substance is the substratum on which properties are predicated. The cartesian substance causes dualism and interactionism, whereas the Aristotelian "substance" causes substance pluralism, which we think is not a problem. It is not a problem because how the substance is understood does not lead to a problem of interactionism. The lower-level is constrained by the higher-level substance's powers to execute rather than physically realize the function assigned to the constituent parts. Higher-level events, tropes, and powers can thus be interpreted as causal relata for DC.

2.4 Second Objection – Meaning of Causation

The second objection that is raised against DC is that how causation is understood in DC has no consensus about causation. As there are various theories of causation but an explanation with the concept of DC does not pick one single theory of causation and specifically efficient causation so one can say that there is no consensus about causation in DC. We can observe in the literature that formal and teleological cause in Aristotle's set of fourfold causation is usually invoked.

2.4.1 Downward Causation as the formal cause

There are three types of changes (Ross 1929) that occur are briefly and succinctly described by Aristotle. Any change attributed to a thing (in the sense of progress or transition from one state to another) can be one of three types:

- Change is incidental to the change of something else with which it is connected, such as billiard balls.
- Change can be transferred from a part to a whole, similar to how clay is the cause of the pot.
- Change can be attributed to the entire thing in its proper sense.

Change resulting from external factors, usually spatial changes (efficient cause), changes resulting from micro-level to macro-level, bottom-up causation (material cause), and change resulting from macro-level to micro-level top-down causation are the three types of change (formal and teleological cause). If there is a change then it should be explained using Aristotle's fourfold causation to make any explanation complete. The fourfold causation of efficient, material, formal, and teleological causes explains the above three changes. The first two of the fourfold causation are acknowledged by the reductionist paradigm, but not the third and fourth. In general, the reductionist framework on causation does not consider all three changes, but only the first two. The third, which is underappreciated, requires recourse to the concepts of emergence and DC.

In contrast to Platonic dualism, in which the soul is a resident of the world of forms, Aristotle uses his concept of hylomorphism to explain this relationship. The hierarchical capacities of the soul, according to Aristotle's psychology, are nutrition, perception, and mind (Shields 2000). For Aristotle, the soul is the form of the body, and hyle in hylomorphism means matter. In Aristotle's Physiognomonics, the mind's dependence on the body and its influence on the body is well recognized.

Mental character is not independent of and unaffected by bodily processes, but is conditioned by the state of the body; this is well exemplified by drunkenness and sickness, where altered bodily conditions produce obvious mental modifications. And contrariwise the body is evidently influenced by the affections of the soul by the emotions of love and fear, and by states of pleasure and pain. But still better instances of the fundamental connexion of body and soul and their very extensive interaction may be found in the normal products of nature (Aristotle 2014)

We can observe that the mind is not independent and unchanged by the processes going on in the body. This can be shown through a simple example like a person who is drunk or sick i.e. there is a change in the states of bodily processes which changes the mental states. In contradistinction to that, we can also observe that changes in the mental states (as in the context of Aristotle's soul) fear or pain there are changes in the bodily states like trembling as well. Although Aristotle did not have a general problem with DC, the problem of mental causation and thus DC, which is unique to the philosophy of mind in its hierarchy of soul and explanation in hylomorphism, can be traced back to him. Mariuz Tabaczek argues for a similar position of DC as a formal cause in recent literature (2013). Tabaczek argues against efficient causality's causal monism, citing examples of philosophers (Andersen 2000, Silbestein 2008) and scientists (Scott 2007, Green 2018) who used Aristotle's fourfold causation. The formal, structural causation has taken the constraints in contemporary times. We can thus observe the resurgence of Aristotelian fourfold causation. Recently we can see that based on the formal and teleological cause in Aristotle the position regarding causation as constraints is becoming prominent.

2.4.2 Downward Causation as constraints

We should try to understand what vitalism and reduction mean to better understand the above juxtaposition. What are the messages that these concepts are attempting to convey? What is the problem with (Vitalism and reductionism) and what do we lose if we reject something outright? There may be a grain of truth in it. It is important to note that this discussion is historical and represents an important step in the evolution of the concept of DC.

What concerns me is the possibility that we reductionists of today may repeat the mistake of the reductionists of the past by denying true facts to which the vitalists point (Campbell 1974)

Campbell says that we should not make the same mistakes that the reductionists have done by not accepting facts like growth, heredity, and infection which can only be found in the biological domain and not in the physical domain. The discussion of vitalism here was specifically directed against the older concept of mechanism (not new wave mechanism) as clockwork, which has no meaningful relationships (Bechtel, Williamson 1998). As a result of access to biochemistry, the wave mechanism perceived in biology today is vastly different from how it was perceived during Vitalism when the clockwork model of mechanism reigned supreme. The clockwork mechanism is also known as the universal mechanism ("Mechanical Philosophy"), which reduces the universe to only external relations such as matter/corpuscles/atoms colliding and moving while rejecting any internal relations. Second, Vitalism proposes an 'élan vital' that separates the living from the non-living. It was regarded as a vital spark, and it was even compared to a non-physical soul at times. Growth, reproduction, infection, heredity, and totipotency (Medawar 1974) are not observed in the objects of physics. The vitalists were specifically opposed to the clockwork mechanism model, which lacked necessary internal relationships.

To begin with, vitalism's claims were dismissed (Ramberg 2000) because scientific endeavour requires empirical /observable evidence, and the concept of vitalism did not hold up in this regard. There is no such thing as a separate vital entity such as a soul or vital élan. Second, it was rejected because it overburdened the ontology with dualism. Even though vitalism was rejected by reductionists, it contained a kernel of truth, and this gap in our understanding of how novelty and life emerge required an answer. Though necessary, the path of inquiry within a successful scientific methodological purview, specifically a reductionist framework, is insufficient. The reductionist approach has accelerated scientific progress, but a post-reductionist approach is required to explain biological systems (Mazzochi 2008, Bunge1991). How life emerges from non-living matter, or, more importantly, how consciousness emerges from a biological basis, is a hotly debated topic. For the British Emergentists, this inadequacy, namely, explaining novelty in the world using only mechanical principles viz. The universal mechanism was the starting point.

Even though vitalism is no longer a scientific hypothesis, it is still used in traditional/complementary and alternative medicine (CAM) practices (Coulter et al. 2019). The reductionist approach gained dominance after Vitalism's demise in the scientific domain and the explanatory success (of reductionism). Campbell's (1974) argument, that DC is a set of higher-level laws constraining the lower-level laws, has recently taken the position of causation by constraint in DC (Juarrero 1998, 2013).

We develop this idea of constraints in the fourth chapter where we define enabling and disabling constraints as creating possibilities and reducing degrees of freedom. Thus we see that the problem regarding causal relata and the notion of causation in DC has been dealt with in the existing literature. A far more problematic is the relation of dependency of the higher and lower-level than the two problems stated above. The problem of dependency can be elaborated as below. We later develop in chapter four an alternative of inherence which claimed to be a better candidate to explicate the dependency relation between higher and lower-levels.

2.5 Third Objection of dependency relation of supervenience

It is while considering DC we notice that two issues mentioned above of relata and consensus, the 'causation' aspect in DC is primarily criticized. In DC, the 'downward' aspect is completely ignored. The word 'downward' in DC implies a hierarchical structure with higher and lower-levels. The first question that arises is which dependency relation between the higher and lower-levels enables DC. Supervenience, grounding, reductionist identity, substance property, or something else could be candidates for this dependency relation. If used for the explanatory purpose of making the concept of DC coherent, each of these forms of dependence has its own set of problems. According to the principle of supervenience (Kim 1993), no change at the higher-level can occur without a change at the lower-level.

While assuming a supervenience relation, it is possible to argue that DC is possible. Andersen et al. (2000) argue that, just as higher-level causal powers supervene on the lower-level, higher-level causal powers supervene on the lower-level. However, how can one attribute causality to a higher macro level when the change originates solely at the lower-level? If one accepts the dependency relation of supervenience, one must accept epiphenomenal causation. If causal powers on the higher-level supervene on the lower-level, then how should we construe causation between mental states or brain states?

The higher-level is grounded in the lower-level in the case of grounding as a dependency relation. However, rather than being an ontological relation, grounding is primarily a metaphysical explanatory relation. The metaphysical relationship of grounding is supposed to be established based on explanatory priority. For

DC, the concept of 'natural grounding' as it pertains to scientific domains is more intriguing than a metaphysical grounding in terms of priority or normative grounding in terms of ethics. However, because grounding is a non-causal relationship of determination, it is unlikely to capture the concept of 'causation' in DC.

The reductionist paradigm, or identity thesis in philosophy of mind, in general, reduces and eliminates anything above the base levels, also known as 'nothing but ism.' The mind-brain identity theory denies the existence of mental processes. When reduction is understood as successional reduction rather than causally eliminative, it is argued that reductionism is a good heuristic (Wimsatt 2006). What is the point of considering identity reductionism as a good explanation if the identity theory eliminates the explanandum?

The substance-property dependency relationship is important for DC because several theories argue from property analysis, such as Cartesian dualism and emergence, which is defined as the "creation of new properties." The issues begin with defining what constitutes a substance, whether it is something that exists independently of itself, as Descartes claimed, leading to mind-body dualism. As outlined by Kim (2003, 1993), emergent phenomena face several challenges, including the exclusion argument, causal closure, and causal power actuality principle. So the question remains unanswered: if these dependency relations can't explain DC or mental causation, then the dependency relation is objectionable by eliminating the very phenomena that it set out to explain.

2.6 Conclusion and summary

The primary contention of this chapter is that DC is not a misnomer. Regarding causal relata and causation, there is elaborate literature. The dependency relation is a bigger problem than relata or consensus on causation. We started from the two problems viz. problem regarding relata and problem regarding consensus on causation in the literature of DC. We elaborated on various relata like generic events, tropes and powers as candidates for causal relata. Secondly, we saw the revival of Aristotelian formal and teleological cause in explaining DC and we finally observe how formal cause is also used in the sense of constraints.

Finally, we posed the question regarding dependency relation as supervenience precludes downward causation. We can observe from the above discussion of DC that it has distinct meanings in biological sciences (Campbell 1974), general sciences (Andersen 2000), and philosophy of mind (Orilia, Paoletti 2017). In conclusion, Campbell and Juarrero interpret DC as laws and constraints imposed by the higher-level on the lower-level. To explain the notion of causation in DC, Andersen (2000), Tabazeck (2013), and Juarrero (2013) appeal to the Aristotelian notion of formal cause. While objecting to the causal influence in DC, production making is considered causation, but this is not a necessary or sufficient condition for causation in general or DC in particular. The meaning of causation has a family resemblance to formal cause or causal constraints, as mentioned above because the notion of DC overarches over various levels.

The DC relata can be thought of as levels formed by generic events, tropes, or abilities. Causation is defined in terms of constraints causal powers, tropes, and events. Causation is a friendly jumble with various, a) ontologies such as events, tropes, powers, energy, and agent causation, as well as various; b) causation criteria such as production, regularity, constraints, intervention, mark transfer, information transfer and so on.

The third problem with dependency relationships is a major impediment to a successful DC explanation. Various dependency relationships face distinct sub-problems, making the situation difficult, if not impossible. Is there another dependency relationship that could solve these issues, which is an open-ended question?

We have now come to a reconnaissance that we require an alternative relation to supervenience to grapple with the concept of DC as it is not a misnomer and we need to make sense of it. To reach this conclusion that an alternative relation of dependency is required, we examined various dependency relations used to characterize mind-body dependency. We compared and contrasted Emergentists' earlier concept of supervenience with Kim's current concept of supervenience. The Emergentists' concept of supervenience as a new type of relatedness contrasts with the current rigid concept of supervenience developed in the physicalist reductionist framework as "no change at the higher-level without any change at the lower-level." We conclude that the current concept of supervenience contradicts the very explanandum, i.e. the mind's causal efficacy, which it was supposed to explain in the first place. As a result, we require an alternative dependency relation capable of performing this function.

CHAPTER THREE

Reductionism and its problems

The really hard problem of consciousness is the problem of experience. When we think and perceive, there is a whir of information-processing, but there is also a subjective aspect.

David J. Chalmers (2007)

3.1 Introduction

In the previous chapter, we observe that the concept of downward causation overcomes the questions regarding relata as 'generic events', 'tropes' or 'powers'. The second question regarding consensus with regards to the notion of causation is headed towards the revival of Aristotelian fourfold causation. These answers are already present in the literature on downward causation. The third problem which we raised regarding the dependency relation is a bigger threat as supervenience precludes DC. In this chapter, we would like to see in which framework the dependency relation of supervenience arose. We would be seeing various forms of reduction in the metaphysics of science and the implication of reduction in the philosophy of mind.

In this chapter, we contrast two kinds of supervenience the reductionist supervenience based on the principle of parsimony as no change in the higher-level without any change in the lower-level. The second is the Emergentist's supervenience as a new kind of relatedness.

The problem of mental causation that Descartes faced differs from the problem of mental causation that we face today. Descartes' problem is known as 'interactionism' because it requires him to demonstrate how substances with inherently opposing properties can interact causally.

Traditional view: Substance Dualism

According to Descartes mind and body are different independent substances having different properties. These properties are mutually excluding each other. The body has extension, but the body excludes any thinking capacity. The mind has thinking capacity but the mind excluded extension in space. Which led to the problem of interactionism. Two mutually exclusive substances are not in a hierarchy but at par with each other and exist independent of each other.

Premise 1. The mind is an independent thinking substance not extended in space.

Premise 2. The matter is an independent substance having an extension in space.

Conclusion. Two independent substances lead to the problem of interactionism as mind and matter have mutually exclusive characteristics and hence cannot causally interact.

To overcome this problem created from dualism of the mind-body the positivist tradition came up with the monist position of physicalism.

Origins of Physicalism and impossibility of non-physical

The contemporary problem of mental causation stems from the analytic tradition's Physicalist ontology of levels in the unity of science. Positivism and Logical Positivism, which arose from the Vienna circle, advocated Physicalism as a step forward from materialism and a reaction to the then dominant philosophy of Hegelian Idealism because it was completely based on reason i.e. the premise real is rational rather than empirical, observational. The methods of positivism were supposed to unify all sciences, and sentences that couldn't be verified were deemed nonsensical.

The so-called Vienna Circle (Moritz Schlick, together with Rudolf Carnap, Herbert Feigl, Philipp Frank, Kurt Gödel, Hans Hahn, Otto Neurath, Friedrich Waismann, among others) has made especially important contributions to the unified syntax of unified science. Their work has greatly advanced the project of combining physics, biology, psychology, sociology, and other genuine sciences into unified science……. it does not recognize two or more "modes of being" with correspondingly different "methods"; it advocates a monism free from metaphysics; and it thus creates the unified science of physicalism as a logical development of the much-maligned anti-idealistic materialism. (Neurath, 1987)

All sciences are methodologically unified and share the same 'mode of being.' The Vienna circle's evolution from positivism to logical positivism is well-known. The concept of methodological unity of sciences arose from the logical positivist movement. Our main concern is to see how the concept of physicalism has evolved, as the problem of DC arises from the way physicalism is understood. The causal closure of the physical as given by Kim (1993) is a major threat to downward causation and hence one needs to understand where the concept arose from. The concept of physicalism arose in the Vienna circle and was taken to its conclusion concerning the philosophy of mind by Kim (2007). To avoid the existence of non-physical entities in physicalist ontology, physicalism got trapped into 'correlational supervenience' due to the acceptance of supervenience as a dependency relation. Alternative to non-reductive physicalism which regards the higher-levels as micro-irreducible is currently seen as the best alternative between physicalism and dualism.

The two characteristic features (Bedau 2008) of weak emergence are

- the dependence of the macro on the micro.
- autonomy of macro from micro.

Bedau (2008) accepts causal and constitutional reducibility but argues for an 'incompressible' explanatory capacity of weak emergence. We accept not only explanatory autonomy of psychology (e.g. in psychotherapy) but also partial causal autonomy of the psyche given our fourfold analysis of function, unity, property and information (FUPI). The position of non-reductive physicalism excludes non-physical entities like soul and élan vital and at the same time accepts some form of dependency along with some form of autonomy. Such a claim becomes controversial due to the principle of causal closure that only physical entities interact causally, if there is a cause it is a physical cause which creates a false dichotomy of physical and non-physical. Whereas non-reductive physicalism can include other entities which are physical but are micro-irreducible. As stated earlier mind supervenes the physical and due to no overdetermination only the physical does all the causal work. So in such a scenario, we have to give up any form of autonomy as the mind is causally excluded. If we generalize exclusion of mind we have exclusion of all higher-levels as there is causal drainage to the lowest physical entities.

3.2 *Choosing ontology: Parsimony vs Eleatic principle*

What is the ground on which we choose certain entities as existing in our ontology? The reductionists eliminate the mind basing the rationale on the principle of parsimony. Whereas the Emergentists want to explain the role of the mind in our ontology having a genuinely causal role. As against the principle of parsimony which accepts minimum presuppositions with maximum explainability we have the Eleatic principle. The Eleatic principle accepts only those entities in our ontology which have a causal role to play. So we need to contrast and compare both these principles to come up with the best suitable epistemic virtue for our purposes.

What is the basis of saying that the mind has a causal role or does not have a causal role to play in this world? Does the mind exist in our world or is it non-existent as it does not have any causal role to play? Mind is an epiphenomenon given the converse of the Eleatic principle that if something does not have a causal role to play in the world it does not exist. What are the entities that make up our ontology? Two selection principles provide an answer to this question. To determine which entities populate ontology, reductionism in general uses the principle of parsimony or the well-known Occam's razor. We have another contender in this context, which is also used to determine which entities should be considered populating ontologies. The well-known Eleatic principle (Assaturian 2021), as stated by Plato in his work Sophists, is a strong contender. Only those entities exist in our world that has a causal profile, according to the Eleatic principle. A corollary of the same principle is that entities without a causal profile in the world do not exist. For example, when the mind is rendered as epiphenomenal given supervenience it is stripped off from any causal role in our ontology and termed the position of eliminativism. Let us first analyse the Eleatic selection principle.

Physicalist worldview to avoid the Cartesian problem of interactionism came up with the idea of supervenience which culminates in epiphenomenal causation. However, this escape creates a new problem: psychological states exist in some sense, but they are epiphenomenal and causally irrelevant. As psychological states do not have any causal profile in a Physicalists worldview, they do not exist within the framework of physicalism, according to the Eleatic principle. Given that the Eleatic principle is true and that psychological states are epiphenomenal, the reductionist framework, in its haste to avoid the Cartesian interactionism problem, ends up with a problem tantamount to parallelism. Even though there is no causal relationship between psychological and physical states, the concept of parallelism states that they are perfectly correlated (Heidelberger 2003). So we shift our focus to parallelism and see if are there any similarities between parallelism with supervenient causation. The problem with parallelism is that it is unclear how the mind-body correlation became so perfect.

This was explained by Leibniz using the concept of pre-determined harmony (Kulstad 1993). Similarly, in epiphenomenalism, psychological and physical states are intertwined without any causal relationship. The concept and dependency relation of Supervenience explain the perfect correlation. The principle of supervenience states that no change in the higher-level states is possible without a change in the lower-level. As we have seen the Cartesian traditional view in the form of an argument, we can formulate the contemporary view regarding mind-body relations as follows.

Contemporary view: Correlational Dualism

As elaborated above the contemporary view hold that supervenience is the best bet to explain mind-body relation. The idea of overdetermination states that there cannot be two causes of the same effect, one cause takes precedence as justified by Ockham's razor. We can understand the idea of overdetermination with a simple example. Consider that a person is on a trip to the desert for exploring. Two enemies wish to kill this person. So one of the enemies poisoned the water of the traveller so if he drinks the water he will die. The other enemy poked a hole in the water container, so the traveller will die of thirst. So whatever happens whether the traveller drinks the water or not she will die. Either of the causes is sufficient for the death of the traveller. But in the case of actual death, only one of the two will be the causes, which can be found out through a postmortem report given whatever happened. Similarly, there can be only one cause in our case either mental states are causal or neural states causal. If we accept the supervenience relation, then mental states are eliminated as epiphenomenal.

Premise 1. Mind supervenes on the physical given correlational studies.

Premise 2. All causal work happens at the physical level hence mental causation should be given-up due to overdetermination.

Conclusion. Supervenience as a dependency relation leads to the problem of parallelism because mental states exist in non-causal i.e. epiphenomenal realm dependent upon neural correlates of consciousness.

Now we elaborately analyse the reductionist position which gave birth to physicalism and later see what are the problems that emerged because of reductionist methodology in the philosophy of mind viz. the identity theory of mind. As we have seen the origins of physicalism in the Vienna circle as a development over the anti-idealistic materialism, we need to understand reductionism to understand its limitations and its consequences for the philosophy of mind in identity theory.

3.3 Reductionisms: to understand physicalism

A precursor to the dichotomy that natural sciences and social sciences cannot share the same methodology can be seen in the work of Kant. Reductionists argued as we have seen the unity of sciences through the unity of method. It should be kept in the back of our mind that Kant (Nicholls 2010) recognized the methodological distinction between natural and social sciences (Naturwissenschaften) (Geistenwissenschaften). Kant also claimed that explanatory practices in biology were influenced by the final cause (teleology). In his epistemology of biology, Donald Campbell (1974), who is credited with coining the term DC acknowledges teleonomical explanations (Ayala et. al. 1974). Even though there is currently no consensus on the meaning of the term physicalism as defined by the unity of methodology. Physicalism, however, continues to play an important role in discussions of philosophy of mind in particular.

The structure of this chapter is as follows. Firstly, we discuss Carnap's constructionist ontology in the reductionist thesis, as well as Quine's epistemic critique of Carnap's reduction. Then we'll look at other reductionisms, such as Nagel's intertheoretic reduction. Then there's Oppenheim- Putnam's mereological reduction and Kim's critique of mereological reduction. These three are the major types of reductions which lead to the understanding of the concepts of levels the backbone of the book.

Then, in the mind-brain Identity theory, we'll see how the problem of mental causation arose within the Physicalists' reductionist paradigm. Finally, we'll look at how our main concern, Downward Causation, is involved in mental causation and the autonomy of sciences in general. All causal powers rest in the lower-level in the reductionist paradigm, to which the higher-level is reduced. In a reductionist programme, Downward Causation is thus impossible. In chapter six, we will apply the reductionist framework to which this book subscribes, namely Wimsatt's robust reductionism (2006). Just like reductionism uses Occam's razor to remove unwarranted entities from populating our ontology we have another principle for choosing what constitutes our ontology viz. the Eleatic principle.

Downward Causation and Eleatic principle

The genuine cases of emergence require DC due to the Eleatic principle, the question of Downward Causation (DC) arises in the theory of Emergence. The Eleatic principle states that an entity is only real if it participates in the world's causal processes. A higher-level emerges from the integration of a lower-level, according to the emergence theory. The higher-level is epistemically unpredictable and ontologically irreducible to the lower-level due to the nature of lower-level properties. As a result, Emergence creates a hierarchy of levels, starting with the fundamental Physical, which merges into Chemical, which merges into Biological, which merges into Psychological, which merges into Social.

There are two DC problems with such a hierarchy. The first is a general one that applies to all levels of hierarchy in general, while the second is specific to two levels within the hierarchy, namely Mental to Physical causation. The idea of higher-level causation is contradicted by Reductionism, which asserts that all causal powers reside in the lower-levels, and thus the higher-level is reducible to the lower-level. There are two major hypotheses underlying the divergence of these antagonistic programs. a) Unity of science as a working hypothesis advanced by Carnap, Schlick, and Putnam in the reductionist physicalism, logical positivism tradition; and b) Disunity of Science as a working hypothesis advanced by functionalist Fodor (Fodor, 2013), later Putnam (multiple realizability) in the non-reductionist token physicalism, cognitive science tradition.

The Unity of science hypothesis argues for the unity of methodology based on observation of all sciences. This insistence on observation made it positive in contrast with metaphysical statements. All the sciences including psychology and sociology were supposed to be reduced to physics according to this prescribed methodology. On the other hand, the disunity of science as a hypothesis recognized that social sciences specifically are not always amenable to observation and other methodologies such as hermeneutics, and phenomenology needs to be used. Now we will see three major forms of reduction viz. constructivist, intertheoretical and mereological.

3.3.1 Constructivist Reductionism

With the pursuit of analytic philosophy for the sake of distinguishing scientific claims based on observation and metaphysical speculative claims, the notion of reduction arose. The ontological reduction was inferred from the reduction of statements (Carnap, 2005), reduction of theory (Nagel, 1935), or part-whole, mereological reduction (Oppenheim and Putnam 1958). For the understanding of reductionism, Carnap proposed constructionist theory, which defined reductionism as;

An object (or concept) is said to be reducible to one or more other objects if all statements about it can be transformed into statements about these other objects. (Carnap, 2005)

As the linguistic analysis was the most common method of philosophizing, statements from one object had to be transformed into statements from another object before the latter could be considered reducible to the first. The philosophical position of reductive physicalism (also known as Materialistic Monism) is that everything that exists is limited to its physical properties and that the only substance that exists is physical. As a result, it claims, the mind is a purely physical construct that will eventually be entirely explained by physical theory as it evolves. In this way, it bets on science's current success and the reductionist analytic model of science explaining the future. Non-reductionists who are looking for an explanation for mental causation, emergence, and other phenomena see reductionism as controversial.

The critique of Carnap's constructive 'reductionism', which is the second dogma of empiricism, is based on the critique of the 'analytic-synthetic' distinction, which is the first dogma of empiricism. The critique of Quine (2000) states that reduction to such observational statements is not possible because observation is not possible in isolation, but observation is always done in a web of beliefs also known as Quinean holism. So, constructivist reductionism had to face these two problems raised by Quine which undermine the celebrated principle of parsimony used by the reductionists. We now proceed to understand the second kind of reduction viz. intertheoretical reduction given by Nagel.

3.3.2 Intertheoretical reductionism

In his classic book "Structure of Science," Ernest Nagel (1961) lays out formal and non-formal conditions for reducing one theory to another. The theory of emergence, on the other hand, attempts to explain the unfolding of the universe on a grand scale in its broadest sense. Both 'reduction' and 'emergence' have a lot of baggage of meaning attached to them, and they appear to be incompatible.

When the theory of emergence is construed as a thesis concerning the logical relations between certain statements, even though Nagel is a reductionist he admits the essential correctness of the theory when it is construed as a thesis concerning the logical relations between certain statements. When viewed in this light, it has far more applications than proponents of emergence usually claim (Nagel, 1961). Reductionism and Emergence, which are seemingly opposing and incompatible at first glance, are not if we understand non-reductive physicalism as a mitigating ground for both. Reduction attempts to move from wholes to parts, while emergence attempts to move from parts to wholes; both approaches can be mutually consistent (Morowitz, 2004). In plain and simple terms, it can be thought of as perspectives or views from the top or bottom. Here, we'll try to figure out what Nagel means by reduction.

Nagel's notion of reduction

Intertheoretical reduction is attained if theories/laws in one established domain (primary) explain a phenomenon in another domain (secondary) that they were not formulated to explain. The target theory is secondary science, which must be reduced to primary science, which is the foundation.

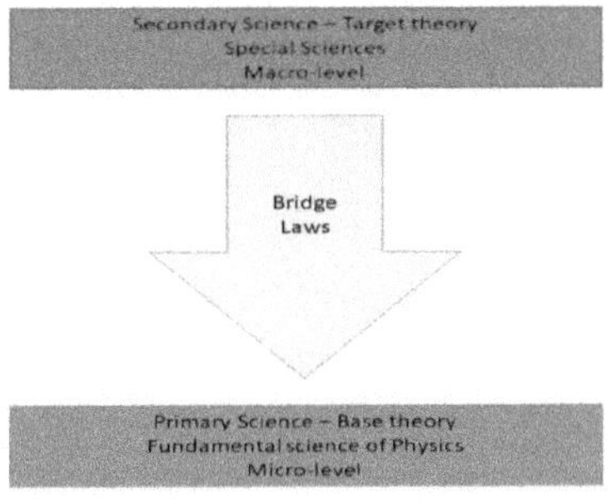

Figure 2 Intertheoretical reduction (Nagel)

The secondary or target theory is reduced by bridge laws to the primary science or base theory which is at the fundamental level of the physical. The nature of bridge laws and the requirement similarity in primary and secondary sciences is stated in detail. We will see the details in formal and informal conditions for intertheoretical reduction.

Two types of reductions

1) Homogenous reductions – In the homogenous form of reduction, the laws of secondary science do not use any descriptive terms that do not have a similar meaning in the domain of primary

science. As a result, the statements of primary and secondary science that have a deductive relationship are homogeneous. For example, the temperature is measured by a thermometer and temperature is the mean K.E. of molecules.

2) Heterogeneous reduction – Between primary and secondary science, there is a qualitative discontinuity in the object of inquiry. Because the province of the theory was designed to handle qualitatively different materials, secondary science has a more diverse vocabulary than primary science. There could be a mereological relationship between secondary and primary science, for example. Primary science is a more fundamental fine-grained micro-level description of secondary science, whereas secondary science is the macro-level whole.

In a nutshell, homogeneous reduction refers to sciences that employ homogeneous descriptive predicates, whereas heterogeneous reduction refers to sciences that employ heterogeneous descriptive predicates. The homogeneous reduction is more epistemic, whereas the heterogeneous reduction is more ontological. There's a good chance that the macroscopic and microscopic phenomena will have a mereological relationship in homogeneous reduction. Some sciences can be reduced in a heterogeneous way but do not have a mereological relationship, such as thermodynamics reduced to statistical mechanics. So, DC will possibly be useful only in the cases of heterogeneous reductions. Let us now see what formal conditions are required for a reduction to be valid.

Formal conditions for reduction

The first formal condition for intertheoretical reduction is that the statements of secondary and primary sciences should be explicit. The axioms, special hypotheses, and experimental laws of sciences must be available as explicitly stated statements, with the various constituent terms having unambiguous meanings determined by codified rules of usage or established procedures appropriate for the discipline (Nagel 1961).

Some questions can be raised in response to the above formal conditions explicated by Nagel. Is psychology and sociology, for example, able to meet this criterion of explicitly stated statements with rules and well-established procedures at par with natural sciences? What is the state of natural sciences, as a result of shifting concepts of mass and gravity? When new evidence is presented, any scientific statement is subject to revision. From Wittgenstein's (language game) and postmodernist (relativism) perspectives, the problem of defining any term as a linguistic entity can be criticized. It is described as the ideal formal situation. The following is a non-exhaustive list of possible statements: a) postulates as a premise, b) theorems and logical consequences of the theory, c) singular statements - the result of observations, d) borrowed laws, and so on.

The second formal condition is an elaboration of the first but attempts to formulate a relationship between the two sciences viz. reduced science and base science. Every statement of a science S can be analysed as a linguistic structure made up of more basic expressions that follow implicit or explicit construction rules. Though these basic expressions may be vague to varying degrees, it will be assumed that they are used unambiguously in S, with meanings fixed either by habitual usage or explicitly formulated rules (Nagel 1961). So are the theories are having some form of a conventional status within the practitioners of that science?

Because there is an explicit mention of usage, the second condition is immune to the criticism that was levelled at the first. The third formal condition is analogous to the middle term in deductive logic. In general, the primary and secondary sciences involved in a reduction share a large number of expressions (including statements) that have the same meaning in both sciences (Nagel, 1961).

There are two sub-conditions to this third formal condition,

a) Connectivity – There should be a link between what is "signified" in secondary science and what is "represented" in primary science by theoretical entities.

b) Derivability condition – The laws of secondary science can be deduced from the laws of primary science using the derivability condition.

Later in the Emergentists tradition, we see various formulations of weak emergence which use the non-derivability or derivability only through simulation (Bedau 1997). Such Emergentist's endeavours are important in developing various forms of DC. We can contrast the non-derivability without simulation definition of weak Emergence with the condition of derivability in Reduction. These connections or linkages can take a variety of forms.

i) Logical connections - The logical connection is established between the meanings of expressions through synonymy or the non-transitive relation of 'analytical entailment,' which asserts that science is logically related to theoretical expressions in primary science. Quine (1976) criticizes the point of 'synonymy' and reduction (to experience statements); we will return to this point later in this chapter.

ii) Conventional connections – Understanding the concept of a "theoretical primitive" is crucial to comprehending this link. A primitive concept cannot be defined using any previous concept or concept. The definition of such theoretical primitives, such as units of measurement, is widely accepted. There should be a coordinating definition that connects primary science's primitives with secondary science's constructs.

iii) Factual/Material Connection – The primary sciences are sufficient or jointly necessary and sufficient conditions for the events or states of secondary sciences, both factually and materially.

All these ways of connections which are in the domains of sciences relate in one-to-one correspondence with the levels of reality, which forms the basis of the upward or downward direction of causation. Not only the direction but these connections define whether the upward or downward causation will be a valid form of causation or a dubious form of causation. Apart from formal conditions, Nagel gives non-formal conditions which apply to intertheoretical reduction.

Non-Formal conditions for reduction

Because Connectability and Derivability are unable to distinguish between trivial and non-trivial reduction as a method, non-formal conditions are required. As a non-formal condition, adequate evidential support for the premises with empirically valid confirmative force, which can be stated as a requirement of 'truth,' should be imposed. It is reasonable to expect evidence, even if the logic of weighing evidence is difficult and unresolved.

The most charitable interpretation of claims and counterclaims of autonomy and reduction is that they are debating which is the most fruitful way to conduct systematic research. The preference is then for the most promising perspective, which is expected to be more fruitful in the investigation and which explanation accounts for the most gains. The seeds of the framework of robust reductionism, which the author adopts later in the book, can be seen here. Given such formal (explicit statements, linguistic analyzability), and non-formal conditions (connectability and derivability) for reduction we need to contrast it with emergence, as only emergent special sciences or levels of reality will be able to exert downward causation or can be debated to having genuine causal influence.

Two versions of emergence

a) Non-predictability version – The properties observed at a higher organizational level are not predictable from the properties of lower-level subcomponents that organize that whole, the condition of analyzability, and derivability is not satisfied, and such phenomena are called emergent, and

b) Emergent evolution version – It is an evolving cosmology in which simpler structures and properties give rise to more irreducibly complex structures and properties distinct from the simpler ones.

Nagel rejects the non-predictability version by arguing that the non-predictable properties are not a part of the vocabulary of that science and it makes no claims about it.

It is undoubtedly the case that a theory of chemistry that in its formulations makes no use of expressions referring to olfactory properties of substances cannot predict the occurrence of smells. But it cannot do for the same reason that mechanics cannot account for optical or electrical properties of matter. (Nagel 1961)

Nagel is of the view that the argument of non-reducibility cannot be based on phenomenal properties because the theory in physics does not have the perquisites of explicit statements. The above quote is crucial in the critique of phenomenal properties-based reductionism. Because phenomenal expressions are not used to express the statements, which is the first formal condition of reduction as seen above, it is impossible to predict phenomenal properties. So the hard problem of consciousness, Mary's room/ knowledge argument, has no solution in reductionism because the first formal condition of "explicit formulation in the form of statements" is not met. The second version of emergence as 'evolutionary cosmogony' is accepted by Nagel. He does warn, however, that there is a difference between emergent in the sense of being temporally novel and emergent in the sense of being unpredictable. Ontological novelty does not have to be temporally/ historically novel. Such new emergent properties and traits, it could be argued, are simply realizations of potentiality hidden in the 'nature of things.' This potentiality could be realized with proper knowledge of the 'nature of things' and correct mathematical techniques. The problem of novel properties is an empirical one that can be solved, at least in theory, by turning to history.

The issues in this investigation are

1) Detailed knowledge of all previous states of affairs in the universe should be known. For such reductions, knowledge of all micro-states is a pre-requisite like Maxwell's demon. Is such an omniscient being possible and if this being is already knowing everything, will such a being engage in science as an enquiry into the nature of the world?

2) The ambiguity of terms like property and process, and the criteria by which we can compare and contrast two processes or

properties. Leibniz's identity of indiscernible is one such criterion that has caused a slew of issues (Black 1952).

3) What distinguishes a novel trait from a reducible trait?

If these questions can be answered, only then Emergence is not a truism for Nagel. Following the preceding discussion, a natural question arises: what is the philosophical or scientific payoff of the reduction theory? According to Kim, there are at least two payoffs. 1) We reduce the number of independent assumptions about the world by reducing one theory to another, resulting in maximum explainability with the fewest assumptions possible. For Occam's razor, the reasons are the same. 2) As a metaphysical payoff for ontological simplicity, bridge laws can be upgraded to identities, resulting in reductive identifications between the higher-level theory and its reducer. We have seen how Nagel elaborately puts forth the ideas of intertheoretical reduction, these ideas when opposed become the very stepping stones for emergence for example non-derivability. We later pose a hard problem of reduction specifically to question the intertheoretical form of reductionism. Now we move ahead to understand the third form of reduction as viz. mereological reduction.

3.3.3 Mereological reductionism

Oppenheim and Putnam in Unity of Science (1958) offer a system of potential micro-reducer. This is helpful in understanding as it serves as a precursor to constitutional reduction as one form of reduction acceptable even in contemporary literature.

The essential feature of a micro-reduction is that the branch B1 deals with the parts of the objects dealt with by B2 related to Pt part-whole relationship and each branch having a universal discourse Um. (Oppenheim and Putnam 1958)

Abiding a list of six preconditions like constitution, mereology etc. for the distinction of levels, the levels are given as,

6	Social groups	Family, governments, nations
5	Living organism	Multicellular
4	Cells	eukaryotic, prokaryotic
3	Molecules	inorganic molecules, biomolecules
2	Atoms	periodic table of elements
1	Elementary particles	Sub-atomic particles or hypothetical strings

Table 2 Mereological Hierarchy (Oppenheim and Putnam)

It is important to note that the psychological mental level isn't included in this list of levels. The mind isn't made up of cells or even specialized neuronal cells as a whole. The mind is a branch of a nested hierarchy that makes up the organism, or individual. The mereological condition of reduction, which requires that the higher-level be decomposable into parts of the lower-level, is the reason for the lack of psychological level in Oppenheim and Putnam. The cellular or even special cells, such as neuronal cells, cannot decompose mental or psychological levels in a mereological sense.

There are some issues with the concept of levels in Oppenheim and Putnam, as a counterexample (Kim, 2010) to possible micro-reducer. According to O-P, the fourth cellular level makes up the fifth level of multicellular organisms. However, an organism contains free radicals, which fall into the second level of the mereological hierarchy. Even though all higher-levels are ultimately reducible to lower-levels, Oppenheim and Putnam claim that levels cannot be skipped in micro-reduction. The above-mentioned counterexample breaks this condition.

As a result, building levels in a mereological manner is difficult. This level problem is further developed in the Framework's next chapter, where various dependency relations that make up levels are discussed, as well as our perspective on dependency, namely the relation of inherence.

In recent literature (Eronen 2015) on "levels", the concept of "scale" is gaining traction in defining the concept of levels. What are the upper and lower bounds of the scale for classifying a phenomenon as mental? The neuronal level cannot be used as a measuring scale because neurons come in a variety of sizes. Because of the mereological fallacy, neither neurons nor the brain is conscious (Smit, Hacker; 2014). Individual people are conscious or unconscious; however, the brain, which is a part of the person, is neither conscious nor unconscious. Individuals, despite being natural entities, come in a variety of sizes based on age and other factors. Even though entities described in physics may have a fixed size, this can be questioned, as an electron can be classified as a particle or a cloud depending on the context of explanation, such as the photoelectric effect or the theory of orbitals. There is no clear boundary between the size of an electron or an atomic scale when considering the smallest and largest atoms and various descriptions of atomic radius such as Van der Waals radius or covalent bond radius. Even well-understood phenomena in physics lack a strict upper and lower bound of scale, so how do we save the common sense description and come up with a scale for mental phenomena? So, even if the scale is used as a criterion for classifying levels, we may end up comparing apples and oranges on the same scale. These can be a few criticisms posed against the mereological understanding of levels. Now we'll look at the implications of the concept of 'physicalism,' which emerged from the previous analysis of various reductionisms and which reductionism is acceptable. All the above reductions are eliminative i.e. they eliminate the higher-levels from the causal nexus within our world. Reductionism in recent literature like Wimsatt (2006)

3.4 Acceptable reductionism

Robust reductionists accept successional reduction and interlevel explanations. The difference between the previously mentioned reductionism and robust reductionism is that the latter rejects causal eliminativism. Only if the higher-level fails to explain the phenomena does successional reduction eliminate it. The phenomenon of success or failure of reduction is not eliminated by interlevel explanation. Robust methodological reductionism acknowledges the phenomenon's causal role in ontology via the explanation, rather than eliminating it. We partially agree with Wimsatt's (2006) thesis regarding the heuristics of levels. We would like to add our concept of mind-body dependency relational inherence between the higher and lower-levels which we have developed in the fourth chapter on the framework.

Type	Successional	Explanatory	Eliminative
Constructivist	✓	✓	✓
Intertheoretical	✓	✓	✓
Mereological	✓	✓	✓
Methodological	✓	✓	✗

Table 3 Kinds of Reductions vs practice of reduction.

If we simplify the kinds and types of reduction, we can observe as depicted in the above table that only methodological reductionism rejects eliminative reduction as ill-conceived and not acceptable. All other kinds of reductions eliminate the higher-level of causal efficacy. How science is practised is argued to be non-eliminative according to Wimsatt (2006).

The framework of physicalism which has been created from reductionist assumptions at least is questionable given the criticisms of reductionism. Constructivist reductionism was as bearing two dogmas of the analytic-synthetic divide and reductionism as stated by Quine. Intertheoretical reductionism is problematized in 3.6.5 further in this chapter given 'hard problem if reduction' viz. reducing Stenberg's theory of love to oxytocin the molecule of love. Mereological reductionism is criticized as there are counter examples

3.5 Identity reduction and elimination of mind

Constructivist, inter-theoretic, and mereological reductions are all general models of reduction that can be applied to the problem of special sciences. Reductionists in the philosophy of mind believe that the mind is made up of brain processes. When the 'is' of identity is defined by constitutional relation, there is no construction or translation involved in identity reduction, but there can be some aspects of mereological reduction. Because it identifies and reduces the mind to brain processes or brain states, the identity theory of mind eliminates the mind. There is no doubt about mental causation in particular and DC in general now that the mind has been removed. The statement "mind 'is' identical to brain states" is investigated in two ways. U T Place is responsible for the first use of 'is' as a constitution but not as a definition (1970). JJC Smart explains the second use of 'is' as a strict identity (1970). Identity reductions eliminate the mind from the causal nexus and accept only the causal efficacy of the neural states. Neural states are important but are they necessary or only sufficient? Is the initiation of causal process qua mental states or brain states? So an understanding of mind-brain identity is of utmost importance for further investigation.

'Is' of strict identity

There are two types of strict identities. Apriori identities, such as '13 is the smallest prime number greater than 12', or a posteriori identity, such as 'this butterfly was the caterpillar.' The identity between the mind and the brain is a posteriori identity. Smart

(1970) argues for a strict identity of mind and brain processes in a series of eight objections and responses. The main argument put forward for our concern is that experience in general cannot be made up of anything or ghostly stuff, but we have studies suggesting mind-brain identity, and it is our best hypothesis based on brain studies. When the mind is identified with brain states, the mind is eliminated from the causal nexus. There is no scope for an explanation of voluntary action. We will see five amongst the multitudes of problems that are created because of the identity theory.

We must define 'composed' in the mind-brain identity theory in a broader sense that allows us to say that indivisible atoms are made up of something other than themselves (Smart. 1970). When the mind is considered non-physical in a dualistic sense, it is equivalent to saying the mind is made up of nothing. Nothing can be constituted or created from something, that can be constituted or created from nothing. As a result, we must assume that experiences are reducible and made up of brain processes in the weak sense. Although the afterimages of experiences are not reducible to brain processes, the experience as a whole is. Similarly, even though the nation is made up of citizens, nation statements can be distinguished from citizen statements. Ontologically, mental states are supposed to be reducible to brain processes, even though semantically, the 'logic of statements' in Smarts terminology can be very different. As we saw earlier, Wimsatt (2006)'s distinction between successional reduction and causal reduction is not clear in 'is of strict identity'. Place views the constitution's identity as a scientific thesis but, Smart claims that identity is a philosophical thesis rather than a scientific thesis. The rationale for identity being a philosophical thesis is that the competitors in identity reduction are concepts such as epiphenomenalism, physicalism, and non-reductive physicalism, which are involved in establishing or rejecting the idea of mind-brain identity.

The mereological reduction of the part-whole type is the 'is' of the constitution. The difficulty with such a reduction is determining which brain 'parts' make up the 'whole' mind, and the candidates range from gross to subtle, including the entire brain, brain lobes, neurons, and quantum microtubules in neurons. Where do we draw the line? Which level is the most fundamental? Where can we say that mind-like properties are visible? The identity theory has squabbled with neutral monists, Panpsychists, Panprotopsychists, and Emergentists over this candidacy. As previously stated, we agree with (Smit & Hacker 2014, Boyle 2017) that the mereological fallacy is correct and that mental phenomena can only be applied to the whole person, not to individual parts such as the brain. Further now a question arises as to how reducibility and irreducibility is characterized in the philosophy of mind.

The type-token distinction and functionalism

a) Type reduction

Every mental type is identical to every physical type, according to type physicalism. Although different mental events may have the same physical correlation, there is a physical event that is correlated with each type of mental event. Pain, as a type of mental event, can be reduced to c-fibre firing, according to the standard example given. In the same way, all mental processes can be reduced to physical processes. As a result, the higher mental level adds nothing to the physical level, and the lower-level processes do all of the causal work. The standard example is that of pain which is realized across species; mammals, molluscs, and reptiles by the same type of underlying mechanism e.g. C-fiber firings. If there is the same kind of neural firing which realizes pain across species like mammals, reptiles etc. then that is called type identity.

b) Token reduction

Token physicalism states that for every mental type token, there is a physical token to which it can be reduced. The multiple realization argument prompted the development of this type of physicalism. Multiple physical processes can realize higher-level properties, according to the multiple realization argument. The software can, for example, be installed on multiple pieces of hardware or even multiple silicon/carbon substrates. In the same way, the mind can be realized in multiple worlds. As a result, because it can accommodate multiple realizability, the token reduction is a weaker version of physicalism. Kim (1992) believes that there are two forms of eliminativism of the higher-level or the mind, the first is complete elimination like the pre-scientific notions of phlogiston and the second is elimination from the causal-explanatory process within the scientific paradigm and nominal existence like tables.

the present view does not take away species-restricted mental properties, e.g., human pain, Martian pain, canine pain, and the rest, although it takes away "pain as such". Second, while the standard eliminativism consigns mentality to the same ontological limbo to which phlogiston, witches, and magnetic effluvia, have been dispatched, the position I have been sketching views it on a par with jade, tables, and adding machines. To see jade as a nonkind is not to question the existence of jade, or the legitimacy and utility of the concept of jade. Tables do not constitute a scientific kind; there are no laws about tables as such, and being a table is not a causal-explanatory kind. But that must be sharply distinguished from the false claim that there are no tables......... Psychology remains scientific, though perhaps not a science. (Kim 1992)

c) Functional reduction

The constitution, according to functionalism, is unimportant, but the role or function played in the system is. Machine functionalism and causal physical functionalism are the two main types of functionalism. Any functional theory is defined by the presence of something that mediates the input and output processes. The input is represented in the brain as a result of the external stimulus. These representations are processed by rule-governed algorithmic operations, which produce output. Given the brain's or circuitry's immense complexity, this output can become an input for subsequent processes in a chain, leading to more output. The concept of machine functionalism is used when the mediating function is similar to a Turing machine, whereas the concept of causal functionalism is used when some complex physical activity, such as the brain, is required. The mind, according to such an interpretation of functionalism, has no causal power. The causal role is played by the brain's computational processes. Because the brain physically realizes mental states, the mind is epiphenomenal to physical processes. The explanation of phenomenal qualia (Nagel 1974 Chalmers 1996) and the inability of reduction to explain semantically (Searle 1984) the content of thoughts, are two major issues that this position faces.

When will psychological states be able to claim their place in ontology? According to the Eleatic principle, psychological states can only be said to populate ontology if they have causal powers. So, once we've established the causal powers of psychological states, we'll be able to secure their place in our ontology. As a result, we present our position of dependent and independent, continuants, and their causal powers in the sixth chapter. The sixth chapter uses an analysis of property, unity, function, and information to argue that the mind is a dependent continuant with causal powers.

3.6 Problems for identity reduction: biology, legal, psychology, logical, theoretical

In 'is of identity' we have seen that the mind is identified with the brain states. If this position of identity is held, then it will face five problems. We enlist these problems stating that non-identical mental states and brain states can be shown by analyzing other components besides the brain states that are involved in mental functioning. Non-identity is also shown by observing that the predicates of the mind are ascribed to the person as a whole and not to brain states as part of a person.

3.6.1 Problems in biology: brainless organisms, phantom limb, gut-brain axis

What about intelligent behaviour of organisms with no brains like jellyfish or unicellular organisms that show intelligent behaviour like moving towards a nutrient gradient and moving away from toxins and poisonous stuff? Not a topic for our book but the Orch-OR theory of consciousness (Hameroff 2012) draws an argument from here against the, only brain is a necessary and sufficient condition for consciousness way of thinking. This idea also goes against the mind-brain identity theory that the mind or consciousness can be reduced to one part of the body viz. the brain.

The next problem in the domain of biology is the phantom limb problem. A soldier in the war was hit in the leg by gunfire. Due to the time lag in transporting the soldier to the hospital and the poisonous nature of gunpowder, the site of injury developed gangrene. His leg was amputated to prevent gangrene from spreading to other parts of his body. The leg would be healed in time, and the amputee soldier would be discharged from the hospital. However, a new issue arose: the amputee soldier was experiencing severe pain, which appeared to originate in the area where the gunfire had struck his leg. The leg is not 'ontologically' present because it has been amputated, but the source of pain is felt in the location of the severed leg. A phantom leg is a leg that does not exist but from which the amputee still feels pain. What impact does explaining this phantom limb phenomenon have on the identity theory of mind? The physical causal closure principle states that all physical effects are caused solely by physical causes and nothing else. The pain in the phantom leg is thought to be caused by firings in the brain. This misfiring is sending a pain signal to a body part that does not exist, the phantom limb. A body part doesn't need to exist to feel pain in it.

Premise 1. All physical effects occur if and only if a physical cause exists.

Premise 2. The phantom limb is the source of physical pain.

Conclusion. As a result, phantom causes can have physical effects.

Pain is a highly subjective, but physical, experience. Naturally, the veridicality of the experience is called into question in the case of phantom limb pain. The brain can generate mental states about something that does not even exist physically. So we must either accept that the brain can generate psychological states of non-veridical experience or accept that phantom causes can have physical consequences. If we accept the preceding statement, the realm of experience extends beyond the physical. If we accept the latter, then the causal closure of the physical is called into question due to phantom causes. Of course, pain is a false signal produced by the brain (Smart) or CNS (Armstrong), but this example demonstrates that identity theory overdetermined the phantom limb experience. Because we do not need a body to experience the body in this exceptional case, we can infer the limitations of rigid theoretical models (Cassandra 2012). This example shows that the correspondence between the brain and body part is not a one-to-one relation, so there is an inherent caveat in the identity theory. The identity theory fails to explain correspondence with biological body parts also. Another problem for identity theorists would be the gut-brain axis which is suggested to be playing an important role in mental functioning e.g. mood.

there is growing evidence that alterations in the gut microbiota may play a role in the pathogenesis and/or symptomatology of major brain disorders, emphasizing a clear need for more investigations to better understand the mechanistic links along the MGB axis (Murciano-Brea, Julia, et al. 2021)

MGB (Microbiota Gut Brain) axis is amassing evidence regarding what role the microbiota in the gut plays in mental functioning. This evidence points towards a rejection of mind-brain or mind-CNS identity in the sense that there are more variables involved than thought by the reductionist identity theory.

3.6.2 Placebo effect: A problem in psychology

Intheir paper, Matthew D. Lieberman et al. (2004) state that the beliefs exert a causal influence over the physical body has a long history comparable to the history of medicine. According to research, placebos bring about changes in brain activity similar to the pharmaceutical medicine they are replacing. The effects of placebo administration are similar to those of active chemical agents. However, it is not known as to which placebo-specific activity influences the consecutive change unique to the symptom in brain activity. Their research is demonstrating that downward placebo effects related to beliefs changes the brain activity regions which are normally affected by other treatments, which through 'placebo induced thoughts' which are top-down. The pharmaceutical medication which are bottom-up causes and placebo both can affect the region of brain but the medication does it directly whereas the placebo does it, whereas placebo effects are usually mediated by placebo-induced thoughts. According to fMRI scans, the researchers believe that placebos operate partially by increasing beliefs about the emotive dimension of pain (i.e. "I believe I will be less bothered by pain now"). They propose a disruption theory to explain how the placebo effect works.

"The reflective conscious processes that are engaged in response to automatic negative affective processes tend to inhibit or 'disrupt' the very same negative affective processes due to a hardwired feedback mechanism." 2004 (Lieberman)

The conscious process of reflecting disrupts the negative feedback mechanism and inhibits pain from the top down. So there are alternative ways of influencing the brain states apart from the physical pathways as given by the disruptive theory of placebo effects.

3.6.3 Habeas cerebrum: A problem in legality

The Latin phrase *"habeas corpus ad subjiciendum"* means that the office personnel detaining the prisoner should present the prisoner's body in front of the court magistrate in legal cases when the unlawfully held prisoner is asked to be presented in front of the court magistrate. Also in legal cases, a person has summoned not the part of the person as in the brain which is doing all the causal activity. If all causal activity for any behaviour is happening in the brain, then who is culpable for legal/illegal behaviour and who is detained? A simple truism is that if the brain does all of the causal work, why bring the entire body? The point I'd like to make is that one of the verification conditions for considering certain behaviour as illegal or legal is that the agent has a body rather than only a brain

– the cerebrum. As a result, the title of this section asks identity theorists whether only the entity involved in a causal nexus of behaviour should be presented to the court magistrate for release or punishment. Verification conditions for determining whether the brain was involved in a criminal act would require entirely different equipment and setups, such as neuroscientists, EEG, or other brain-related equipment. The identity theory fails to explain the social pragmatic concerns of legality where the person is held causally responsible for any act. So either we must state that in the social/legal domain of study causal responsibility of action ascribed to a person works or only one way of explaining i.e. the causal chain of brain states is correct.

3.6.4 Sufficient and necessary conditions: A problem in logic

INUS conditions in their full form are insufficient but necessary components of unnecessary but sufficient conditions (Mackie 1974). To grasp the concept of INUS conditions, Mackie provides a standard example. Assume a house caught fire due to a short circuit. In this case, because there is no flammable substance present, the short circuit cannot cause any combustion. So, in addition to gasoline (or any other fuel), a short circuit resulted in the house catching fire. The short circuit, as well as the fuel, are required conditions in this case. Even though it is one of the necessary conditions, a short circuit is insufficient. As a result, fuel, as well as a spark from a cracker, cigarette lighter, or matchstick, could serve as a necessary cause. In Aristotelian terms, the necessary cause is an unintended cause that happens to be a cause in a given situation.

In the context of INUS conditions, two arguments could be used. To begin with, consider the mereological fallacy argument: in this case, the brain is a sufficient condition, but other supporting conditions of the 'whole' are assumed, such as providing food and oxygen to the brain, sensory input to the brain, and motor input-output from the brain. Later on (Boyles 2017, Dewey 1988, Hacker 2014), rather than identifying the mind solely with brain processes, the case for the mind existing in the body/person is advanced. The famous multiple realizability argument is the second argument that can be used in this context. Although brain processes are sufficient for the mind, mind-like phenomena can be realized in principle by a variety of physical processes, including computers, so the brain is not a required condition. There are creatures without brains, such as jellyfish, and unicellular organisms that show intelligent behaviour such as moving toward nutritional gradients and away from toxins. Alternative modes of enacting intelligent behaviour are possible, making the brain a sufficient but not necessary condition for the human mind. This again casts doubt on the strict identity theory, which assumes that brain states are both necessary and sufficient for mental states to exist.

> .... the supervenience relation, the supervenience of the mental on the physical is marked by the fact that physical states are causally sufficient, though not necessarily causally necessary, for the corresponding mental states. That is just another way of saying that as far as this definition of supervenience is concerned, sameness of neurophysiology guarantees sameness of mentality; but sameness of mentality does not guarantee same ness of neurophysiology. (Searle 1992)

Searle in 'The Rediscovery of the mind', according to the above quote states that given the dependency relation of supervenience the neuro-physiological states are sufficient for the mental states to exist. At the same time given the concept of multiple realizability, the neuro-physiological states are not necessary and some other physical substratum can do the same causal work.

This non-necessity of substratum suffices to reject type identity. If some particular substratum is not necessary for realizing a higher-level organizational property but can be in principle replaced by another substratum, then the higher and lower cannot be type identified. This is tantamount according to Searle to say that if there are the same neuro-physiological processes there would be the same mental processes even though the same mental processes can be realized by multiple substrates. We contest this claim that Supervenience faces a problem, if we hold this as true the same neural processes will cause the same mental processes given recent studies on pain.

Pain is considered a subjective feeling realized by neural processes. Recent studies have shown that social pain and physical pain have overlapping neural processes (Eisenberger 2012). This leads to our formulation of the converse of the multiple realizability thesis which we term 'polymentation'. The concept of polymentation states that multiple i.e. poly, mental states, i.e. mentations, can be realized by the same physical substratum. We have words like polysemy in linguistics or polypotency/ pluripotency in biology which suggest a similar idea in that specific field like our concept of polymentation.

Premise 1. Social pain and physical pain are two token mental states.

Premise 2. Social pain and physical pain is realized by overlapping neural states.

Conclusion. If two tokens on higher-level have one token of realizer, then token identity is not true.

So the same token brain state can realize multiple mental states which goes against the supervenience relation. So we not only reject type identity but also token identity. This argument not only questions the identity like multiple realizations but now questions the dependency relation of supervenience itself.

Supervenient/epiphenomenal causation accepts that multiple realizability grants some form of irreducibility to the higher psychological level. Even though some form of irreducibility is granted it is of no use as the psychological level has no causal powers of its own but mental states inherit causal powers as mental states supervene on physical states. According to the causal inheritance principle - CIP given by Kim (1993) mental causation is reducible to physical causation. Mental states inherit some form of a faux or pretend causation.

There are no token causal powers other than those occurring at the microphysical level. The only hope for special-scientific causation rests on higher-level properties staking a claim to the causal powers of microphysical properties (Hannikainen 2010)

Hannikainen states that given the relation of supervenience and that token physicalism is true the only hope for any higher-level causation is doomed to be at stake only on the microphysical level causal powers. Now that we are stating that token physicalism itself is questionable so we have a better chance of explaining higher-level causation given both multiple realization and polymentation. Hence we need another relation of dependency which we find in the concept of inherence which is discussed in the fourth chapter of the framework.

According to Searle, the irreducibility of the mind is because of how we use our language. He states the eliminative reduction of higher-level to the lower-level is because we have an appearance and reality distinction. A phenomenon which subjectively appears to us is reducible to the lower-level which is observer-independent real e.g. subjective feeling of heat reduced to mean molecular motion. The higher-level which is given in appearance is not real and hence can be eliminated. But in the case of consciousness or mental states what we have is only appearance and we are unable to make the appearance – reality discernment as consciousness which appears to us is a reality in this case. But this irreducibility does not have much bearing because all the causal work is done by the physical processes and consciousness as the word used in our language is necessarily subjective.

> .... Consciousness is not reducible in the way that other phenomena are reducible, not because the pattern of facts in the real world involves anything special, but because the reduction of other phenomena depended in part on distinguishing between "objective physical reality," on the one hand, and mere "subjective appearance," on the other; and eliminating the appearance from the phenomena that have been reduced. But in the case of consciousness, its reality is the appearance, hence, the point of the reduction would be lost if we tried to carve off the appearance and simply defined consciousness in terms of underlying physical reality (Searle 2008)

We ask for a new problem in the vein of the hard problem of consciousness named by the author as the 'hard problem of reduction'. This supposedly would be a big problem for identity reduction.

3.6.5 Hard problem of reduction: A problem in theory reduction

Is it possible to reduce ontological complexity? Take, for example, the so-called love molecule, phenyl ethylene amine/oxytocin, which is explained at the neuro-hormonal level (lower-level). The neuro-hormonal system, according to reductive physicalism, is at a lower-level. While Sternberg's famous love theory has a phenomenal level of popularity. According to the reductive physicalist, the phenomenal level is supervenient. Sternberg's triangular theory of love is an explanation for the phenomenon of love at the individual level (higher-level). Now, at a lower-level, phenyl ethylene amine, in combination with dopamine and norepinephrine (biochemical components), causes ecstasy and uncertainty, resulting in insatiable desire, which is referred to as love. While intimacy, passion, and commitment (phenomenal components) are the phenomenal components of Sternberg's theory, the dynamics in these factors lead to a specific quality of love. Both are explanations for love; the question is which one is the catalyst. Is it true that certain behaviours cause the release of hormones, or that certain behaviours cause the release of hormones? Hormones and neurotransmitters allow for the possibility of love, but engaging in certain behavioural patterns causes neurotransmitters to be released. Which hormone, or a combination of hormones, could be responsible for feelings of intimacy, commitment, or passion? It's a difficult question to ask for bridge laws connecting neurotransmitters and phenomenal aspects of love, which we call the 'hard problem for reduction.' Further, asking to ontologically reduce love to neurotransmitters, when each neurotransmitter has a plethora of functions, is arrogant. It's a two-way street: the presence of biomolecules allows for certain behaviours, and engaging in those behaviours causes biomolecules to be released. As a result, it is a mutual rather than an asymmetric causal relationship. Thus reduction of the theory of love to the theory of hormones is a hard problem that reductionists will have to face.

Given myriads of problems due to reductionism can we use reap the benefits of reduction without facing the unintended consequences of elimination? We will look into this aspect in detail in chapter four where we draw our framework from Wimsatt's work on robust reductionism. To evaluate and select appropriate forms of reduction useful for our framework presented in the next chapter, we analysed the principle of parsimony and the Eleatic principle. The Vienna circle, in opposition to Idealism at the time and one step ahead of materialism, developed Physicalism as an ontology. Physicalism was arrived at through reductionist methodology, given the principle of parsimony. The various forms of reductions can be classified into three broad categories: constructivist, intertheoretical, and mereological. The constructivist reduction faces the problems stated by Quine (1976). The intertheoretical reduction faces the hard problem of reduction, reducing the theory of love to a hormonal explanation. The mereological reduction faces the problem as stated by Kim that one cannot skip a level while reducing. Finally, we present the methodological reduction position, which maintains the virtues of successional and intertheoretical valid reductions while rejecting eliminative reduction. The analysis of ontology selection principles leads us to the conclusion that eliminative reduction is, to use Wimsatt's (2006) terminology, "ill-conceived".

How does one interpret what over determines what? So will the person in the desert die because of water being poisoned or the non-availability of water? The question is whether the person's death occurred qua poisoning of water or non-availability of water. Similarly, in the philosophy of mind, we ask did the action occur in qua mental states or brain states. Rather than the principle of parsimony which has led to the reductionist methodology, we think that the principle of charity as an epistemic virtue will be a better selection criterion.

The principle of charity is an epistemic virtue

Reductionism as a strategy relies upon the principle of parsimony. As seen in the third chapter we have various problems which reductionism is fraught with. We had prominently seen five problems specifically created due to the reductionist identity theory of mind. To overcome these problems, we need to rely on epistemic virtue viz. principle of charity. The principle of charity is an epistemic virtue when interpreting a certain statement or a position taken in the form of a group of statements. The principle states that when we have two competing interpretations one should grant the most suitable rational interpretation amongst the competing two. While we apply this principle we should not ascribe fallacious reasoning, falsity or illogical reasoning when a competing rational interpretation is possible.

When natural language is used to describe scientific truths they often seem contradictory like in the example of scientific statements, that one can never touch anything and the sensation of touch is the repulsion of electrons. While on the other hand, we have a scientific claim that the solar probe named parker has touched the sun. We are led into the discussion naturally as to what is truth. should we take the meaning literally or with a pinch of salt? How do we interpret this meaningfully without being incoherent? Of course, according to the context, we know both statements are true, but at the same time, both assertions are opposite. According to the Cambridge school of analysis (Stebbings 1932), these are the criticisms of the common sense language philosophers within the linguistic turn on the artificial language philosophers of the logical positivist tradition. Moore (1925) had given the distinction between 'understanding a proposition' and 'knowing its analysis'. According to this distinction I exist, I move my hand are examples of understanding even though one cannot give its analysis. C. D. Broad the Emergentist, Wittgenstien, Stebbings were all members of this Cambridge school of analysis. Whether a given analysis is correct or useful is dependent and relative to the purpose why one seeks such analysis.

We have a strong contender in the principle of charity as an epistemic virtue in contradistinction with the principle of parsimony. How do decide whether brain states over determine mental states or not? If we accept parsimony over charity, then the one will answer the qua problem as brain states are causally efficacious. If we accept charity as a virtue over parsimony, then one will answer the qua problem as mental are causally efficacious. So the context plays an important role in determining what has played a causal role in bringing forth an action.

3.7 Conclusion and summary

We went about how physicalism as a thesis sprung from the three reductionist positions constructivist reductionism of Carnap, intertheoretical reduction of Nagel and mereological reduction of Oppenheim and Putnam. This background led to the reductionist identity theory in the philosophy of mind. Identity theory, we have argued, violates the symmetry property of identity. If a = b, then b = a, according to the symmetry property we can interchange the sides in an equality/identity. So, if the mind is the same as the brain processes, then the brain processes are the same as the mind, according to the symmetry property. Unless the principle of symmetry, which is characteristic of identity, is violated, one cannot be eliminated while the other remains intact. However, because the identity theory eliminates the mind, it is debatable in light of the property of symmetry and ontology selection principles based on the Eleatic principle.

We discussed the five problems that are created by accepting an identity theory of mind. The first biological problem asks, how biological organisms without the brain show intelligent behaviour, how the phantom limb creates pain and what is the role of the gut microbiome apart from brain states in mental functioning. The second is the problem in psychology as to how placebos work. Is there a belief-based disruptive pathway apart from the standard neural pathway? The third is a problem from the legal domain as to who is culpable for an illegal or legal act the brain states which are the part of the person or the person as a whole.

The fourth problem is that of necessary and sufficient conditions. The multiple realizability argument asserts that while brain processes are a sufficient condition, they can theoretically be realized in a variety of processes, such as computers and hence not a necessary condition. We conclude from the existing arguments, first, that identity theory ignores other sufficient conditions such as blood supply, sensory input, and motor output, and instead focuses on only one of the sufficient conditions, namely brain processes, which is problematic.

We added our concept of polymentation where for example social pain and physical pain, more than one mental state can in principle be realized by the same brain states thereby rejecting strong supervenient dependency. Multiple realizability creates a problem for type identity whereas polymentation creates a problem for token identity. Finally, we pose the hard problem of reduction. We do not ask to reduce sensory states (non-derivability of olfactory senses etc. from neurophysiological statements) to brain states. Neither do we ask qualia to be reduced to brain states. But we ask could Stenberg's theory of love be reduced to oxytocin the so-called hormone of love.

CHAPTER FOUR

Framework of Inherence, Reduction and Ontology

There are four species of movement—locomotion, alteration, diminution, growth......But if the essence of soul be to move itself, it's being moved cannot be incidental to it, as it is to what is white or three cubits long; they too can be moved, but only incidentally—what is moved is that of which white and three cubits long are the attributes, the body in which they inhere; hence they have no place: but if the soul naturally partakes in movement, it follows that it must have a place. Aristotle(1984)

4.1 Introduction

In the second chapter, we saw that an alternative dependency relation is required as the contemporary definition of supervenience precludes downward causation. In the third chapter, we have seen the details and major problems along with unintended consequences that eclipse the methodology of reduction. Thirdly we need to represent the ontological status of the mind as we have seen it does not have any ostensive referent.

Three major philosophical positions form the background and framework within which the book is made coherent. Firstly, the framework and the notion of dependency relation pose an alternative of inherence (Patterson 2017) against the contemporary view of supervenience. The second component of the methodology is robust reductionism, which is based on Wimsatt's (2006) work. We examine and conclude these positions, weighing their explanatory superiority over competing theories. Thirdly ontological framework is elaborated based on Basic Formal Ontology (BFO).

The mind, as " *res cogitans*", is an independent substance that does not exist in space, according to non-physicalist dualists. While the body res extensa, which is governed by the laws of mechanics, is a self-contained substance with the necessary property of spatial extension. As a result of one substance being extended in space and another not existing in space, the problem of explaining how they interact is known as the interactionism problem. Naturalists such as the British Emergentists avoided the interactionism problem by avoiding supernatural non-physical entities such as the soul or *Elan vital*. Within the Emergentist paradigm, the mind emerged from the underlying processes, but the mind still has causal efficacy, according to the Eleatic principle. The mind is reduced to and identified with the body in physicalist monism, or it is a function of bodily processes. As a result, the mind has no causal role in reductionist and functionalist explanations. As a result, reductionist and functionalist explanations face the tragedy of denying the mind's explanation as inert, ineffective epiphenomena.

Non-reductive physicalism is a pluralist synthesis of the non-physicalism thesis and physical monism antithesis that is gaining in popularity. Kim has stated in several papers that non-reductive Physicalists will face problems such as causal closure, causal exclusion, and downward causation if she accepts the causal efficacy of the mind. Kim devised epiphenomenal causation to avoid these issues while still providing a logically consistent account of the mind in our ontology. All of the causal roles are played by lower biological processes in epiphenomenal causation, and the mind is related to these lower processes through a modified relation of supervenience. The epiphenomenal causation account is based on the supervenience realization dependency relation, which we will see now.

The concept of inherence was used by Aristotle in antiquity and Patterson (2017) in modern times to characterize the mind-body dependency relationship. We examine this relationship and propose additional missing details to establish it as a valid relationship for describing mind-body dependency. The earlier notion of supervenience as a new kind of relatedness is developed further which is somewhat analogous to the configurational forces of Emergentists.

The laws of motion themselves do not place any limit on what kinds of forces can operate on bodies so, if there are forces which can only come into being when matter achieves a certain level of complexity, all that classical mechanics requires is that the motion produced by these forces should conform to Newton's laws. So, if we understand downward causation in terms of configurational forces, then the existence of downward causation is not incompatible with the laws of mechanics. (Crane 2001)

The Emergentists argued for configurational forces which emerged by complex relations between the relata. If the relata do not have any internal relations or complexity built into it then as a heap it will have different properties. No laws are violated if configurational forces are understood in this way. But if there are complex relations between certain relata then it will have distinct properties from such a heap. The distinction between a heap and a complex whole is termed resultant and emergent.

There is a distinction made between relational and compositional inherence. The identity theory, on the other hand, did not make such a distinction and instead relied on the supervenience relation. The higher-level, we argue, is found in the relationships between the parts rather than the parts themselves. At the same time, there is a subtle difference between Aristotle's formal cause, which emphasizes the relationship of form as a whole to the external rather than the relationships between the parts. We claim that internal relations among the parts, rather than external relations, are what gives the form as a whole its unique unity and identity, based on further unity analysis. This inherence relation can be used as an alternative framework for making downward causation a logically coherent concept. In the light of the above discussion now we would look into the relation between supervenience and the problem of correlation dualism which is created by accepting the supervenience thesis.

4.2 Supervenience – root cause of correlational dualism

The use of the concept of Supervenience in the British Emergentism period and the contemporary period is vastly different. Naturalism was the framework in which the British Emergentists worked. Natural explanations rejected supernatural entities and explanations such as soul and vital élan. Naturalism was thought to be pious, but not in the religious sense of the word. There is a difference in the usage of the word supervenience in emergentist literature and the contemporary philosophy of mind literature.

Stress should again be laid on the supervenience of new kinds of relatedness (cf. XL), which are accepted, on the evidence, with natural piety. From the point of view of emergent evolution, we should not say that the relatedness observable in the crystal is implicit in the solution, but that there are lower kinds of relatedness therein which are involved as the physical basis of crystallization. So, too, we should not say that mind is implicit in life, or life implicit in Matter, but that vital relatedness is involved in the natural genesis of mind and physico-chemical relatedness is involved in the natural genesis of life. (Morgan 1925)

The term "supervenience" was used to refer to a "new type of relatedness." One should not that the relatedness for example the snowflake is implicit in the liquid state of water. Analogous to that one cannot say that the mind is implicitly present in life or life is somehow present in the matter already. This usage of the word supervenience is in stark contradiction to the contemporary usage of the word. The contemporary meaning of supervenience as no change in the higher mental level without any change in the lower neural level entails an impossibility of emergence and downward causation.

As a result, supervenience had a specific connotation, namely, an emerging higher-level with a new type of relatedness. Physical entities, as defined by physics, are unquestionably physical; however, are physical relationships between physical entities also physical? Relationships between physical entities are purely coincidental. Relationships are not non-physical in the sense that they are supernatural for naturalists like British Emergentists. Relationships are a natural part of life, but they are also contingent. It is well-known to argue that relations are physical because their ontological existence differs from that of physical entities. The British Emergentists wanted to make the simple point that unrelated physical entities are resultants when grouped. Emergent physical entities are related physical entities with novel properties. If relations are to be called physical, they must be ontologically equivalent to physical entities. However, the recent definition of Supervenience as stronger, weaker, or global has nothing to do with relatedness at the lower-level. Supervenience is an ontological dependency relation that precludes emergence by defining the higher-level as epiphenomena. The term "supervenience" refers to a deterministic dependency relationship.

> A-properties supervene on B-properties if and only if a difference in A-properties requires a difference in B-properties—or, equivalently, if and only if exact similarity with respect to B-properties guarantees exact similarity with respect to A-properties. (McLaughlin, Bennett 2005)

This stipulative definition lays the foundation for a deterministic dependency relation which essentially debars the A level from any causal efficacy whatsoever. Is it possible for physical entities' properties to change as the higher complex acquires new properties? The properties of the lower-level entities do not change; what changes is the relationship between them, which shifts from being unrelated to being complexly related. When stating differences in B properties, the concept of supervenience does not specify what kind of difference is being dealt with. Do the properties of atoms change when they are part of a molecule or when they are part of a cell? Is the supervenient base – realized the higher-level difference in one-to-one correspondence or exponential or like the butterfly effect?

The origins of the misunderstanding that arises from the concept of supervenience must be investigated for clarity in the reductive identity. The contemporary definition takes this stance to avoid the phenomenological fallacy. The after image of an object, such as the shape and colour of a rose, is expected to be formed in the brain as identical to the shape and colour of the rose in phenomenological fallacy. The brain scans, on the other hand, only show correlated electrical activity in the brain with no after images. These experimentally verified facts about brain correlations are sufficient to conclude that CNS activity is required for any higher-level mental processes. The deterministic dependency relation of supervenience was formulated because any change in the lower-level electrical activity is required for any change in the higher-level phenomenal mental activity. There can be no change in X without a change in Y, just as there can't be a change in the higher phenomenal mental level without a change in the lower neurophysiological level.

The phenomenological fallacy states that there are afterimages in the mind equivalent to the properties and objects found in the external environment.

> there is, in a sense, no such thing as an after-image or a sense-datum, though there is such a thing as the experience of having an image, and this experience is described indirectly in material object language, not in phenomenal language, for there is no such thing. (Place 1959)

To avoid the phenomenological fallacy, that there is no internal theatre in the brain the reductionists went too far. Claiming necessity was fine, but the reductionist took it a step further, identifying the mind with the brain, reducing the mind to brain processes, and declaring the mind epiphenomenal. Reductionists who go too far to avoid the phenomenological fallacy fall victim to the mereological fallacy. The mereological fallacy ascribes the predicates of the parts to the predicates of the whole. Individuals' predicates are ascribed to the part of the individual, the brain, in this case, due to identity. Only the electrochemical processes in the brain are linked to the psychological predicates that should be attributed to the individual as a whole. In other words, in mereological fallacy, the properties which are only attributable to the whole are misattributed to the parts. When a deterministic relation claims identity by reducing the higher-level to the lower-level, this is exactly what supervenience demands. The bottom-up supervenience relation appears to be appropriate for certain correlation explanations. The supervenience relation, on the other hand, prevents the emergence and, due to the mereological fallacy, misinterprets the higher-level whole as reducible to lower-level parts. As a result, another relationship must be found for the top-down explanation. Only a relation of supervenience, according to Kim (2007), is physicalism close enough to avoid many inconsistencies within the mind-body problem.

Supervenience, therefore, looks like just what the nonreductive physicalist has ordered: It promises to be a nonreductive dependency relation that can do justice to both her physicalism and antireductionism. The thesis that the mentality of an organism supervenes on its physical nature seems to capture both the physicalist requirement that mentality depends on and is determined by physical properties and the antireductionist thesis that this dependency falls short of reducibility. Note the following important point: Although supervenience perhaps doesn't imply reducibility, it need not be taken to imply irreducibility either-- that is, supervenience suffices for the purposes of the nonreductive physicalist if it is consistent with both reducibility and irreducibility (Kim 2007).

According to Kim supervenience is the solution for maintaining a physicalist ontology while at the same time allowing some kind of irreducibility. Even though according to the above quote supervenience is enough for both reductive and non-reductive according to Kim, supervenience renders the causal influence of mental states as epiphenomenal. According to the converse of the Eleatic principle, that which does not have any causal role to play in the world is eliminated from the ontology.

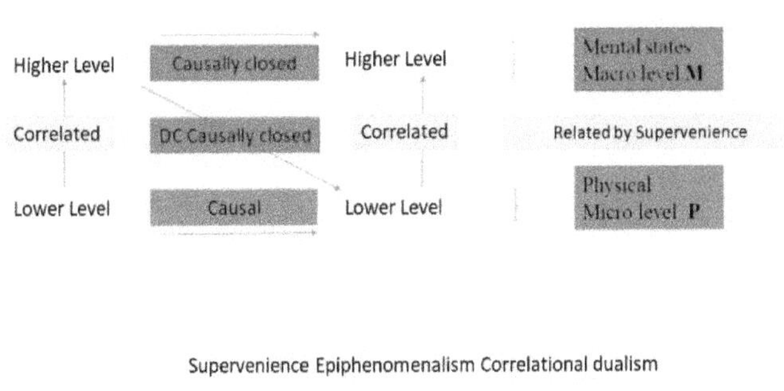

Figure 4 Correlational Dualism

This leads to our main concern of the book termed 'correlational dualism'. Through the relation of supervenience, we have preserved the irreducibility of the mental states at the cost of giving up the causal profile of the mental states. The mental states are correlated and occur parallel with the neural correlates of consciousness but have no causal efficacy. So ultimately supervenience is of no use to explain the causal efficacy of our intentions. How is the supervenience relation a solution to the mind-body problem if it denies the mind's causal efficacy? Given the Eleatic principle, if the causal efficacy of the mind is denied, then the mind as an explanandum is denied as having any ontological status.

Characteristics of correlational dualism

- Accepts some form of non-reducibility of the higher-level.
- The higher-level has no causal profile, rendering it an epiphenomenon.
- Higher and lower-levels are always in synchrony (occur parallel to each other).
- The lower-level has a causal profile.

This makes the same level of mental causation impossible and also makes mental downward causation impossible.

the higher-level phenomena are taken to 'arise' from and depend on the processes of the comparatively lower-levels and ultimately, on processes at the fundamental level. This dependence is usually not taken to be of a causal kind, but to be a form of supervenience together with some form of asymmetric determination. Namely, it is not only held that there can be no difference in the mental phenomena without some difference in the physical phenomena, but also that the latter phenomena are responsible for the former being what they are, and not the other way round. (Mayr 2017)

The relation of supervenience is 'asymmetric determination' because the lower-level determines what the higher-level will do but its converse the higher-level determining the lower is not possible making DC impossible. If supervenience has such problems and a dependency relationship is required. Is there any alternative to supervenience that avoids the problems of causal closure and exclusion while preserving the mental realm's causal efficacy? As stated in the quote preceding the beginning of this chapter, the so-called soul responsible for movement resides in the body through the relation of inherence, as stated by Aristotle himself. The Aristotelian theory of hylomorphism, in which hyle refers to matter and morph refers to form, is well-known. The concept of hylomorphism is discussed in depth, as well as various types of unities, including hylomorphic unity. There is no detailed analysis of the relationship between Inherence and Inheritance in Aristotle or recent works (Patterson 2017). In the section on compositional versus relational inherence, we elaborate on the characteristics of the Inherence relation, drawing on Aristotle.

4.3 Inherence: Mind is dependent on Person – Framework I

Now we discuss the warranted part of the argument of our book as a whole. Is there a viable alternative to the supervenience relation, given its failure to explain the causal efficacy of the mental psychological level? To avoid overdetermination, the discussion of hylomorphism (Aristotle) suggests that, rather than characterizing the mind-body relationship as the mind supervening on the body, an alternative account of the relationship is required. We saw in chapter two on misnomers that Aristotle's views on causation, namely formal cause and teleological cause, are invoked to explain the phenomena of DC. The relationship between soul and body, according to Aristotle's ideas, is one of inherence. The inherence relation's specifics are sparse, we elaborate on the relation of inherence and develop it in the terms of 'relational inherence'. Patterson (2017) recently defended the relationship of inherence in contrast to Emergence in his thesis Emergence and Causal Powers. Patterson argues that non-reductive inherence is a better fit for explaining phenomena than the explanatory concept of Emergence. All physical objects are open-systems and porous, according to Thebolt (2013). We argue that the so-called causally closed physical is causally porous given various active and passive powers. Ellis (2012) makes a similar claim, claiming that there is a causal slack at the micro-physical level. The microphysical forms the necessary conditions, while the macro level has sufficient conditions in the form of macro-level causal powers. Wilson (2011) makes the same claim, that macro-level entities have a subset of the physical's causal powers.

4.4 Relational inherence vs constitutional inherence

We have seen identity reduction based on is of the constitution in chapter three on reduction. The brain states are identical and that is what constitutes the mind eliminating any form of the non-material entity as the mind. The is of identity is correct in eliminating the non-material, but it leads to the qua problem of whether the causal work is done by the mental states qua brain states or mental states qua mental states. For this purpose, we suggest an alternative dependency relation of inherence which can afford dependency as well as causal efficacy to the mental states. Constitutional inherence is a dependency relation where the higher-level properties depend on its constituent relata. Relational inherence on the other hand is a dependency relationship where the higher-level depends on the relations between the relata at the lower-level. The lower-level constituents are sufficient but not necessary for the existence of the higher-level.

The 'relations' of the lower-level components make up the higher-level, not the properties of the components that make up the lower-level. We can specifically get rid of two major problems concerning the mind by using the relationship of Inherence in the robust reductionist framework:

1) coherence with multiple realizability, and

2) the debate between physicalism and nonreductive physicalism.

The formal cause of Aristotle's hylomorphism, which makes no distinction between relational and compositional forms of inherence, is not the same as the Inherence relation posed here. The structures in an inherence relation are created from internal relations to the whole, not just the form as a whole. Apart from the external relations among the parts that make up the external form, the structure gains causal powers due to the autonomy gained through the involvement of semantics, functionality, and environment. The higher-level is found in the 'relationships' between the parts, not in the parts themselves. As a result, the higher-level can be distinguished but not separated from the parts. John Dewey (1988) also suggests a mind-body inherence relationship, but he does not elaborate on what constitutes inherence.

This idea will become more clear with an example, clothness inheres in the thread in the sense that thread is the material cause of the cloth, this is constitutional inherence. Now imagine that there are multicoloured threads by weaving them in an intricate pattern we get a beautiful design of a peacock. The peacock inheres in the relations between the threads and not in the threads per se. The peacock on the cloth resides in the bearer cloth with the relational inherence dependency relation. In principle, there is plasticity in the sense that the threads can be unwoven and a new design can be created of a tree, parrot or whatever. Now the thread can be cotton, nylon or wool which is multiple realizability of clothness. Clothness is a sufficient condition for the design, in the sense that no design is also a plain design. Any design could have been chosen to be woven with the threads available, which is more important than analogical reasoning for the thesis.

The psychological system's higher-level structure, Apophenomena, is a dependent yet partially autonomous distinguishable level that has acquired causal powers. The prefix 'Apo' stands for detached, derived, and dependent, while phenomena refer to the object of awareness in experience. In contrast to causally inefficacious epiphenomena, epiphenomena are detached and derived yet the dependent object of experience that is causally efficacious due to partial autonomy. Words like an apology and other words with the prefix 'Apo' have similar meanings, so Apophenomena isn't a strange term. Second, the higher-level does not exist in a Supervenience dependency relation with the lower-level. Supervenience is a dependency relation that states that if a higher-level Y is dependent on a lower-level X, then Y cannot change without X changing. Emergence and downward causation are not allowed under this stipulative definition.

The Inherence relation, on the other hand, can better depict the relationship between higher and lower-levels. The higher-level is embedded in the lower-level relationships, not in its parts. In formal logic, we have a distinction between matter and form, where the subject and predicate make up the matter and the copula determines the form of a proposition. Similarly, in the real world, the matter is what makes up the physical, but the relationships between matter determine the structure and form of the objects or processes that exist. The copula does not have any reference (syncategorematic) in the real world as the subject and predicate might have a reference. As analysed in the sixth chapter using the concepts of property, unity, context, and function, the higher-level is not separable from the lower-level, but only distinguishable from it. Both the higher and lower-levels exist at the same time. However, functionality and interaction with the environment gain partial autonomy and, as a result, causal powers of their own as a result of semantics. To conclude inherence is a weaker relation than supervenience which can tolerate multiple realizability and polymentation. At the same time helps understand the dependency between the lower-level and higher-level emergent structure.

4.4 Robust reductionism: non-eliminativism - Framework II

Successional reduction and Interlevel explanations are accepted by robust reductionists. The point of disagreement between earlier mentioned forms of reductionism and robust reductionism is that the latter does not accept causal eliminativism. Successional reduction eliminates the higher-level only if the higher-level fails to explain the phenomena. Interlevel explanation of success or failure does not eliminate the phenomena. Robust methodological reductionism does not eliminate the phenomena and acknowledges its causal role in ontology via explanation. In this book, we do partially agree with Wimsatt but additionally, give our relation of Inherence between the higher and lower-level.

We utilize this feature of robust reductionism specifically in the case of mind which is token reducible but not type reducible and hence cannot be eliminated. Robust reductionism states that the eliminativist notion of reductionism is ill-conceived. Dependency on the lower-level which cannot be rejected given various studies is acknowledged by the non-reductive physicalist. While at the same time partial autonomy and explanatory powers of the special science also need to be given due credit. In the sixth chapter where we engage in function, unity, property and information (FUPI) analysis the author claims a partial autonomy of the mental states. Our next framework is Basic Formal Ontology (BFO) which has its roots in the work of Aristotle's categories and the work of W. E. Johnson.

Aristotle's categories for a realist ontology

The mind conceptually assorts sense data in an a priori manner into categories, which is the broadest form of classification possible. According to Aristotle, substances are entities that presumably lie beneath all of our predictions. The category is not only a linguistic entity, but it must also correspond to the experienced world in a broad sense. In this sense, categorized entities must correspond to either particulars or universals in the experienced world. We saw Descartes' definition of substance as a thing that exists independently itself in the literature review section. Aristotle defines substance as about which properties are predicated. Keeping these two opposing definitions of substance in mind, we proceed to explain the Cartesian error of substance dualism. The error is in claiming that the substance is independent. The characterization of substance from predicates leads to a plural world which according to Aristotle interacts with perception (Marmodoro 2014). Such an Aristotelian characterization of substance is distinguished from other substances according to sortal conditions and not independence. Recent development based on the Aristotelian categories and Johnsons' (1921) occurrent and continuant classification is conceptualized as Basic Formal Ontology (BFO).

4.5 Basic Formal Ontology: Representing existing entities – Framework III

A precursor to the origins of basic Formal Ontology is the distinction between 'identity of adjectives' and identity of substantives due to Johnson (1921). The 'identity of adjectives' is given by logical conjunctions while the 'identity of substantives' is given by its manifestation in space-time. The substantives or existents are further classified as continuants and occurents. A continuant continues to exist even though its parts/states or the relations between parts/states change. While on the other hand, occurrent is usually a process.

Basic Formal Ontology (BFO) was first developed by Smith and Grenon (2002). BFO was developed as a top-level ontology such that it could categorize entities in a domain-independent manner. BFO has two broadest categories occurrent and continuant, in which all existence can be classified without reference to specific domains of sciences. Along with his team, Smith has developed various ontologies top-level, mid-level and domain-specific ontologies. The mid-level ontologies are sub-categories within the broadest of the categories namely continuants and occurrents. While the domain-specific ontologies are built in collaboration with knowledge domain experts e.g. gene ontology, specifying subcategories within mid-level ontologies.

Basic Formal Ontology (BFO) is independent of specific domain for categorizing universals, entities, objects, qualities or processes. This framework is developed by Arp, Smith and Spear (2015). What is ontology, is the first question that arises for BFO. The word ontology is derived from the Greek root 'on' and its genitive case 'ontos' along with the modern Latin 'ontologia', which means being or existence. In ontology, we classify and state what exists. The category is the broadest form of classification possible where the mind conceptually assorts sense data in an a priori manner. Substances, one of the categories according to Aristotle are entities which presumably lie underneath all our predications. The category is not only a linguistic entity but in a broad sense has to correspond to the experienced world. In this sense, the entities which are categorized have to correspond to either particulars or universals within the experienced world. Ontology in BFO is defined as

A representational artefact, comprising a taxonomy as proper part, where representations are intended to designate some combination of universals, defined classes and certain relations between them. (Arp, Smith and Spear 2015)

For BFO ontology is a human representational structure where the universals or classes are classified into most general categories. The reality, as we think and express it in our language, makes knowledge 'knowledge' when sharable in an intersubjective manner. So, we have reality or truth tied to our thought processes which are tied to language. We do not go into the debate of fictional objects, non-existent objects or numbers as linguistic entities and restrict ourselves currently to the point that language, thought and reality are intertwined. So, the broadest classification is created from this usage of language.

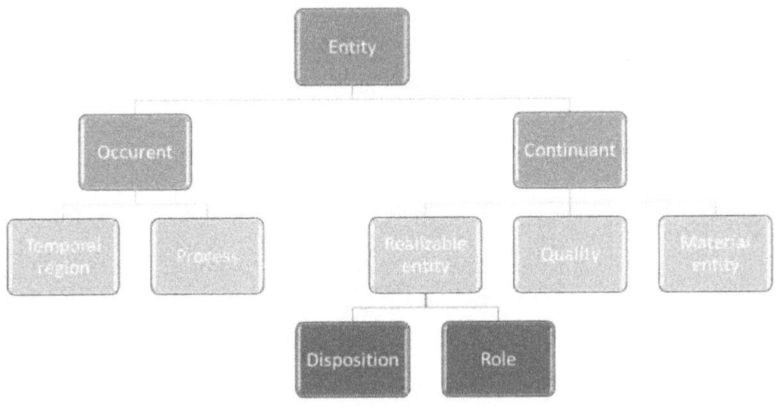

Figure 5 Basic Formal Ontology (BFO) and realizable entities.

In the above image, we have a representation of upper-level ontology and where realizable entities fall in the structure of BFO. Realizable entities are situated under the broader category of continuant. Mind and mental states are considered realizable in the brain states. We will be using this framework of BFO later in chapter six to criticize the identity theory stated in the third chapter. An important question to ask as we are interested in whether the mind has a causal or not, do occurents and continuants both have causal powers or not.

Causal role of occurrents and continuants

Cncerning the causal powers of occurrents and continuants, Simons and Melia (2000) argue that occurrents do all causal work and continuants do not because continuants are not fundamental. In contrast, the author contends that we must understand the sub-categories within dependent continuants. The argument for causal efficacy only ascribed to the occurents is based on occurents being fundamental. This argument from fundamentality is tantamount to micro-reductionism (Mumford and Anjum 2017) which is already criticized in the literature. There is no valid explanation as to why should it necessarily be the case that occurrent is fundamental. We have to explain though under what conditions continuants have causal powers. Having BFO as a domain-neutral framework we use this framework in the specific domain of psychology in the sixth chapter when we discuss and critique Mental Functioning Ontology (MFO) due to Frishkoff (2012).

4.6 Conclusion and summary

In this chapter, we set forth the framework in which we can coherently make sense of downward causation. For this, we choose three background overarching concepts. Firstly, the concept of Inherence where we distinguished between relational and constitutional inherence. Secondly, we discussed the concept of robust reductionism against the reductionism done by identity theory which eliminates the mental states from causal nexus as seen in the third chapter section 3.5. Finally, we discussed the framework of Basic Formal Ontology (BFO) which we later use to represent the nature and ontological position of the mind within the wider classification of existing entities.

CHAPTER FIVE

Downward Causation in Self-organizing systems: the problem of self-causation

...even the one body system has a basically non-mechanical feature, in the sense that it and its environment have to be understood as an undivided whole, in which the usual classical analysis into the system plus environment considered as separately external is no longer applicable... (Bohm 2004)

5.1 Introduction and Motivation

In chapter two we saw that DC faces multiple problems because of which it is suggested that DC is a misnomer. One more problem that DC faces is known as the problem of self-causation. In the case of levels of hierarchy, the higher-level is dependent upon the lower-level. If the higher-level has to exert a causal influence on the lower-level it seems absurd because the higher-level is dependent for its very existence on the lower-level. To answer this problem, we suggest that if one views causation as constraints rather than production, we will not face the plight of explaining the absurd in the case of DC viz. self-causation.

Enabling constraints are bottom-up causes that create the possibility of something existing. Disabling constraints limit the system's degrees of freedom and narrow its choices, which are structural, functional, and meaningful relationships that assign executive roles to the parts. We discuss causality as enabling and disabling constraints in this chapter to critique the absurdity of transitivity in causal relations. We argue that if downward causation is viewed as causation by constraints, it will avoid the absurdity of self-causation caused by the transitivity principle. Organizationally new structures emerge from the system's lower-level subcomponents during the self-organization process. Such self-organizing systems are sui generis and transcend the transitivity principle by causally influencing their subcomponents. Downward Causation refers to higher-level systemic constraints that causally influence the components in a self-organizing system without violating any physical laws.

We contend that by considering causation to be non-transitive, we can avoid the absurdity of self-causation. There has been a great deal of research into the problem of causal closure and causal exclusion of the mental or higher-level in Downward Causation (DC). Among the problems that DC faces, the absurdity of self-causation is a less-explored area. This chapter focuses on the problem of self-causation, which impedes DC coherence, rendering it absurd and thus removing the higher-level from any causal nexus. The cause is always before the effect in time. If we try to trace this causal nexus back to the beginning of time, we should come across the first cause, assuming infinite regress as a fallacy. This first cause will be self-caused, or 'sui generis' self-caused. Causation is primarily conceived of as a material cause in such a metaphysical analysis. Given the transitivity of causal relations, the effect can't be the cause of the cause in the material causation sense of causation. Transitivity states that if A, causes B and B, causes C, then A is the cause of C even if B is the immediate cause of C. Given the transitivity relationship, C can't be the cause of A or B.

"How is it possible for the whole to causally affect its constituent parts on which its very existence and nature depend? If causation or determination is transitive doesn't this ultimately imply a kind of self-causation and self-determination an apparent absurdity" (Kim 2010)

As previously stated if we trace causal nexus to the beginning of time, the infinite regress argument provides a metaphysical reason to accept the first cause as sui-generis or self-cause. The absurdity of any other cause (other than the first cause) being a self-cause is due to causality's transitivity and asymmetry. How is mental causation possible in the case of the mind, which is dependent on lower-level neural processes, because something dependent cannot have any causal influence over which it depends due to the transitivity of causation? Given that neural processes cause mental states; how can mental states have any causal influence over neural states given the asymmetry of causality? We will look at two examples where causal relationships exist but the causal properties of transitivity and asymmetry do not. This encourages us to look for alternative methods of causal efficacy other than production making or material cause sense of causation. This leads to the constraint interpretation of causality as enabling and disabling constraints that can tolerate violations of causality's transitivity and asymmetry.

Two examples of causal asymmetry could be given: a) two books standing against each other (Mumford and Anjum 2011) and b) a tree being the cause of leaves and leaves being the cause of the tree (Juarrero 1998). In the first example, book A is argued to be the cause of book B standing at a 45-degree angle, while book B is argued to be the cause of book A standing at a 45-degree angle. At time t, book A encourages book B to stand, whereas, at time t*, book B encourages book A to stand if the causal asymmetry implies a time lag in the causal relationship. Causal asymmetry means that if A is the cause of B, then B cannot be the cause of A; if B can be the cause of A, then A and B have causal symmetry. However, in the case of the books, there is a common cause which is an external organizing force, someone who has arranged the books to stand against each other. However, when the books are left to their own devices, the law of inertia keeps the books in a state of rest, which is the cause of the books standing in this manner. The point is that in this case, some external organizing agent was required for this to occur. However, the inertia of one book acts on the other book simultaneously and not asymmetrically. As a result, when the inertia of one book and the inertia of another book manifest at the same time, they become simultaneous causes for the other book to stand at a certain angle. Because of simultaneity, the asymmetry of causality is violated.

The tree produces the leaves in the second example, so the tree is the cause of the leaves. Photosynthesis in the leaves produces food, allowing the tree to grow and thrive. Even though the leaves are dependent on the trees for survival, they do have a causal influence on the tree's growth. This causal influence is not diachronic but occurs concurrently. Given the preceding two examples, the leaves in this case are dependent but still have a causal influence that does not result in absurdity.

Given the spontaneous organizational nature of self-organizing systems, there is no external agent (billiard ball model of causation) or substantial (in the case of mind) self that can be entirely attributed to having 'The' causal influence. The paper addresses two issues: 1) whether self-causation is truly absurd, and 2) whether event ontology of causation is appropriate for expressing mental causation. It is argued that self-organization can overcome the absurdity of self-causation and that constraints ontology is far superior to event ontology of causation. The absurdity of self-causation is based on the transitivity of causal relations. Second, the ontology of the event [x, P, t], where x is any existing entity or object and P is a property displayed at time t, requires that x be an object or entity if physicalism is true. When the object or entity is not a monolithic whole, viewing causation ontology as a constraint is superior to events ontology.

According to Kim (2010), the entire 'M' is formed by the constituent parts P (P1, P2... P_n) and the relation R between P1, P2... P_n. The mind is realized by the physical and is dependent on it through the supervenience relationship. To establish mental causation, the mind must causally influence the physical on which it is dependent. To cause something is to create it or bring it into existence. This is only in the sense of the term "material cause." The problem of self-causation arises from the assumption that all causation is production making or bringing forth.

Debates about emergence and DC have gained prominence in recent times within the domain of Philosophy of mind due to retrod discourse in complexity theory, self-organizing systems, and thus the possibility of explanation within scientific Physicalists' perspective (O'Connor and Wong 2002). DC is a debatable concept due to many inconsistencies such as causal closure, causal exclusion, and violation of the causal power actuality principle. Mental phenomena are causally excluded and eliminated from the Physicalists point of view due to the principle of causal closure that all causation is physical. According to causal closure, if there is a cause, it must be physical, and anything non-physical, such as the soul, is causally excluded from the Physicalists' reductionist programme. Because the causal exclusion argument excludes the mind from the physical domain, reductive physicalism is also known as eliminative materialism. Simply put, physicalism holds that everything is physically formed (Mellor and Crane 2002, Kim 1992) and that all causal interactions are physical (Kim 1992, 2007). Causation should involve physical events $[(x, t) P]$ according to Kim (200X), fundamental forces according to Papineau (2013), and fundamental or non-fundamental forces according to McLaughlin (2019) such as Van der Waals forces or London forces. As a result, Physicalists establish the above stringent conditions for DC acceptance.

Physicalism in this sense (which way-state reference) excludes the mental as having no causal influence, leading to eliminativism and epiphenomenalism. As a result, physicalism creates a false dichotomy that divides reality into acceptable physical and unacceptable nonphysical. Because of this dichotomy, non-reductive physicalism has become appealing. Non-reductive physicalism is a variant of physicalism that accepts the higher-level as broadly physical but not narrowly physical (Bennett 2008). The explanation of mental phenomena by reductive or non-reductive physicalism is one of the major debates in the philosophy of mind.

5.2 The Physicalists and Naturalists' troubles with substantial dualism

The problem of interactionism called into question the traditional Cartesian view of the mind as an independent substance. According to Cartesian dualism, the mind is an independent thinking substance and matter is an independent substance with extension. According to interactionism, the mind, which is a substance with no extension, cannot interact with matter, which is an extended substance. The British Emergentists attempted to resolve this issue by positing the mind as an emergent entity from a new type of lower-level relatedness. The British Emergentists were naturalists who eliminated supernatural entities like the soul or Elan vital. To support their claim of a new type of relatedness, they proposed the concept of configurational forces to explain the causal efficacy of these emergent entities. However, no configurational forces were discovered, resulting in the demise of the British Emergentists (McLaughlin 2019).

Rather than viewing the mind as a separate substance or emergent entity, identity theorists equated it with brain processes. The mind, according to identity theorists, is the brain process. Identity is an equivalence relation that is reflexive, symmetric, and transitive. The relational property of symmetry is violated by the identity theory of mind. If $x = y$, then $y = x$ according to the symmetry property. If according to identity theorists, the mind is the brain, then the brain is also the mind according to the relational property of symmetry. On identity alone, the morning star cannot be reduced to the evening star, nor vice versa; however, both are nominally (not ontologically) reducible to Venus. Identity theorists reduce the mind to brain states and eliminate them causally. As a result, there is no symmetry, and the corollary of identity theory that the mind is the brain does not apply to identity theorists because only the brain exists ontologically, not the mind. So the elimination in identity theory does not abide by the property of symmetry which is an important property of identity.

The mind's reliance on the various brain and bodily processes is well documented, as evidenced by various scans and fMRI studies (Bassett and Gazzaniga 2011). The problem of self-causation arises as a result of such dependency relationships. Self-causation is illogical because it violates the asymmetry property of causal relations. Asymmetry implies that if x causes y, y cannot be the cause of x. How can the mind influence the brain/body to cause any behaviour if the mind is dependent on and caused by brain/ bodily processes? There can be no mental causation because of the asymmetry of causal relations. Mental causation includes both mental to physical and mental to mental causation. As previously stated by the problem of self-causation, mental to physical causation is problematic because the mind is at a higher-level and physical brain/body processes are at a lower-level, which is the cause of the mental. According to the physical realization thesis, mental to mental causation necessitates the involvement of a physical realizer, which is DC. We are concerned with the root problem, also known as the DC problem, which is mental to physical causation. To understand how can the concept of self-organization overcome the problem of elf-causation we first need to understand what is self-organization.

5.3 Characteristics of self-organization

Self-organizing systems fall somewhere between the reductionist assumption that order is created by transferring it from an external system and the religious dogmatism that order is created by external supernatural entities. Self-organization is defined as organization traced back to interactions between components, where nonlinear interactions between elements can be amplified by positive feedback loops to create attractors that result in the emergence of new patterns of order. This new pattern of order can be viewed ontologically as a mark of a new level, while metaphysically it can be viewed as a substratum for new traits or properties. These self-organizing processes necessitate that the system is far from equilibrium for new randomness, fluctuation, and noise to succeed and take hold as emergent patterns. When a system is far away from equilibrium, it can enter a complex state (the edge of chaos) that allows it to create new phenomena and regenerate itself for long periods of time through self-organization. Every dynamic system is part of a larger system and is thus interconnected with the top and bottom, as well as the elements that comprise it, forming a complex network. Bottom-up and top-down feedforward/feedback loops can be viewed as complementary rather than opposed. Bottom-up and top-down feedforward-feedback loops can thus be compared to redox reactions, but because these loops emerge far from equilibrium, they are much more dynamic.

> Self-organization is a process where a system reproduces itself with the help of its own logic and components (i.e. the system produces itself based on an internal logic). Self-organizing systems are their own reason and cause, they produce themselves (causa sui) (Arshinov and Fuchs 2003)

A self-organizing system is an autopoietic (auto means self and poesies means producing) in the sense that it self-reproduces and maintains its existence in the face of entropy. The system's parts and components are replaced, and the structure is kept far from equilibrium. Thus, the parts are contingent, but the self-organizing structure is relatively long-lasting and stable in comparison to the system's parts. The functions are carried out by the parts following the causal constraints imposed by the higher-level structure. The physical parts are physical tokens on which the structure is dependent. As a result, the structure is only token identical to its parts and not type identical. Token physicalism is a non-reductive form of physicalism, not strong physicalism. As a result, self-organizing systems exhibit token physicalism and are thus non-reductively physical. How are self-organizing systems and Emergence related to each other is there an overlap?

5.4 Relation of Downward causation with Self-organization vis-a-vis Emergence

The system requires a causal role in the world for genuine Emergence, which can be explained by the concept of Downward Causation. There are many parallels between emergence and complexity science. Genuine emergence cases attribute causal efficacy to the emergent macro level. As previously stated, DC refers to the higher macro level exerting causal efficacy over the lower-level. Genuine emergence cases attribute causal efficacy to the emergent macro level. As previously stated, DC refers to the higher macro level exerting causal efficacy over the lower-level.

Complexity science seeks to explain precisely those natural phenomena that appear to involve emergence; the range of phenomena covered by complexity science is roughly as broad as examples of apparent emergence in nature (Bedau 2002). Thus, self-organizing systems are related to DC in genuine cases of emergence in which systems exhibit causal efficacy. Questions like what is life in, Biology? What is the mind in psychology? Basically, what is the distinction between a heap and an organized system? There is an overlap between emergence and complexity science in the sense that both seek answers to such questions.

5.5 Causation as constraints

There are numerous accounts given to explain the concept of causation (Kutach 2014), such as regularity, intervention and manipulation, probabilistic, counterfactual, and process. Causation is a category of human understanding according to Aristotle and Kant. Hume, on the other hand, rejects causation in favour of a 'regularity theory,' whereas Russell claims causation is a relic of a bygone era and that laws of uniformity must be replaced by 'Laws of change.' Each account has its own set of advantages and disadvantages. The Probabilistic account of causation, for example, can account for the randomness inherent in nature but fails to explain why the necessary relationship exists. Physical explanations, such as mark theories or energy transfer, can explain why the relationship exists, but they cannot explain mental causation. Because intervention and manipulation require an intervening agency, they have a very anthropic explanation for causation. As a result of such issues, philosophers are moving toward causal pluralism. Causal pluralism regards causation as a cluster concept, a friendly jumble of various attributes (Godfrey-Smith 2010). Whatever the terminology, we must comprehend and explain the change. Even though causation is formal ground, i.e. a philosophical hypothesis in knowledge, it is not a superstition; without it, we cannot make sense of anything, as Mario Bunge puts it (Bunge 1959). With the discussion given above, we can safely conclude that causation is not as Russell says the myth of a bygone age.

It is difficult to define causation as having a single characteristic feature that excludes all others. Various causal notions in science, such as conservation laws, stability, determinism, locality, and extremum principles (Ben-Menahem 2018), support a pluralistic view of causality. Various constraints in the given domain of investigation can be regarded as causal in nature, and these families of constraints constitute causation. These scientific causal concepts define the possibility of space within which some space is actualized. "Constraints are alterations in the probability distribution of a system's state space" (Juarrero 1998). There are two kinds of constraints: 1) Enabling constraints - Constraints that allow the existence of a specific structure or pattern. Actuality implies the possibility of something, and constraints actualize one of those possibilities. Enabling constraints are bottom-up or material causes that create the possibility of this something existing. It is irrelevant whether or not that something is realized, but the realization is theoretically possible. These are typically bottom-up constraints that allow for higher-level existence. Natural laws, extremum principles, symmetry, locality, and conservation laws (Ben-Menahem 2018) enable the existence of entities and processes in the world. 2) Disabling constraints - Constraints based on pruning laws that reduce degrees of freedom and narrow the system's choices (Juarrero 1998). Some possible pathways are rejected, particularly by negative feedback loops, and only a subset of the possibility space is chosen. As a result, a system's pathways are coerced and narrowed down to take specific paths to correct the negative feedback. Top-down constraints are structural, functional, and meaningful relationships that assign executive roles to parts. Bottom-up and top-down causation are thus represented by the complementarity of enabling and disabling constraints. This is not mysterious, and it does not require any non-physical soul or élan vital to explain. The important point is that this explanation does not lead to higher-level nihilism because they play a top-down causal role. As a result of the Eleatic principle, that which has causal power exists, and thus the higher-level maintains its existence in the natural world's causal nexus.

5.6 Higher-level constraints as DC

According to Campbell, teleonomy, or the goal-directedness of a system, is admitted to be true while teleology, or some kind of inherent purposefulness, is rejected. Higher orders organize the real units of lower-levels, such as molecules, cells, tissues, organs, organisms, breeding populations, species, and ecosystems. The latter, which is a higher organization of the former, are facts rather than arbitrary combinations. The reductionists emphasize two points. 1) Higher-level processes are constrained and must conform to lower-level laws, and 2) higher-level teleonomy requires lower-level micro mechanisms for execution. Campbell claims that these two points of reductionism, while necessary, are insufficient and that two more principles, specifically for biological systems, are required. These are 3) The Emergentists principle – The laws of selection that operate in the biological realm are not given by the laws of physics or organic chemistry, or any other substitutes or current approximations of it. 4) Downward causation - The laws of a higher-level selective system influence the distribution of lower-level events and substances in part. This means that the lower-level must conform and is constrained by the laws of the higher-level. For example, in contrast to the worker ant, the soldier ant's jaw is designed and specialized for piercing enemy ants and termites. However, because the antlers are so large and multipronged, the soldier cannot feed himself and must rely on workers. The soldiers' jaws and the distribution of protein within them necessitate the explanation of certain sociological laws centred on the division of labour and social organization. With this, he advocates DC which is characterized by restraint rather than assigning autonomy to higher-levels. So, in addition to the necessary reductionist methods and conditions, Campbell added sufficient emergence and DC principles. Thus, higher-level societal constraints act downward on the individual ant, determining the protein distribution and jaws of soldier ants (Li Tian 2014).

Living systems are autopoietic systems that self-maintain and reproduce. For survival, development, and reproduction, living systems take some paths and avoid others. By avoiding certain paths, the degrees of freedom of the possible paths to be followed are reduced. When a system performs independent operations under certain conditions, it is said to be operationally closed, and the system can be identified as performing those specific operations (Varela F J 1997). These possible paths are referred to as degrees of freedom; the system selects one of the available pathways. Autonomy is classified into three levels based on degrees of freedom: minimal, sensorimotor, and strong (Negru 2016). The metabolic functions that create the organism's identity result in minimal autonomy. The far from equilibrium metabolic processes are kept going in the face of entropy's ability to create equilibrium. Sensorimotor autonomy is found in organisms with higher functions because they can interact with their surroundings using sense and motor organs, giving them more degrees of freedom. Sensorimotor autonomy excludes cognitive and metacognitive abilities, which contribute to a strong sense of autonomy. The living system of agents in strong autonomy can control and is aware of the degrees of freedom exercised. The higher-level constrains the system variables in strong autonomy rather than degrees of freedom as positions in state space. The higher-level contextual constraints limit the available degrees of freedom of the constituent parts of the living system that conform to the higher-level specifications. Thus, self-causation is not an absurdity to be overcome, but rather the very nature of the structure in self-organizing systems.

5.7 Conclusion

The self-organization framework has no particular inclination towards reductionism or antireductionism because it is about networks and relationships in which reducible parts without any external agency or centrally located internal agency give rise to a global pattern. This global pattern in a nested hierarchy is global in terms of its parts, but it is part of the higher super system in terms of its whole. As a result, being a subsystem is relative rather than absolute. However, any structure is dependent on the parts as defined by token physicalism; self-organizing systems can be regarded as non-reductively physical in nature. Ben-Menahem (2011) and Juarrero (1998) claim that construing causality as constraints demonstrates causal relations as constraints. This concept of constraints relegates the production-making aspect of causation to the background. The counter examples of tree leaves (Juarrero), books standing against each other (Mumford, Anjum; 2011), and books standing against each other counter the paradox of self-causation in DC by loosening the condition of transitivity from causation. The higher-level exerts a causal influence without violating any laws imposed by bottom-up constraints, so DC does not violate causal closure and is not subject to the absurdity of self-causation. Thus, constraints can be used to explain both the higher-level of mental science (psychology) and the higher-level of special science in general. Thus, in response to the Physicalists' material eliminativism, the higher-level has causal efficacy in self-organizing systems, according to Naturalists.

CHAPTER SIX

Causal Powers and partial autonomy of mind

Self-knowledge including the ability to use mirror is no more mysterious than any other topic in perception and memory. It is an everyday topic in cognitive science not the paradox of water becoming wine.
Steven Pinker (1997)

6.1 Introduction

In the previous chapter, we saw that downward causation faces the problem of self-causation and how one can reply to it if one accepts constraints as causal. Before that, in the second chapter of the literature review, we saw whether downward causation is a misnomer or not. With the analysis done in the earlier chapters, we can see that DC is an interesting but easily twistable concept, if not used with precaution can lead to debatable conclusions. Till now we were mostly concerned with the metaphysics of science and sparingly philosophy of mind. With this chapter, we would like to specifically enter into the domain of, philosophy of mind. We pose questions such as what is the nature of the mind, if the mind is dependent on physiological processes how can the mind avoid overdetermination? Basically, how can the mind have causal powers of its own, making the mind a respected resident of our ontology? If we can show that the mind has causal powers, then

DC is assured. What is the nature of causation, that itself is a big problem? To simplify the discussion, we condense the debate into two approaches causal nominalism and causal realism.

6.2 Causal relation

There are two major approaches to perceiving causality based on whether one considers that causation as a relation is, mind-independent or mind-dependent. The position of mind-independent causal powers or causal realism is due to Aristotle. While the position of mind-dependent causality is due to Hume. This distinction leads to two opposing views regarding ontology causation. The mind-dependent position is called the nominalist position, whereas the mind-independent position is called the realist. One should keep in mind that causation is a weaker relation than determination and a stronger relation than correlation.

6.2.1 Humean view of Causation

The major threats that DC faces are because of the way how causation is understood in the Humean ontology. Hence it is important to know how Hume construed causality. In Hume's epistemology, there are two sources of knowledge: impressions and ideas. Through sense impressions, we come to know the 'matters of fact' regarding the contingent world. While through relations of ideas we come to know necessary logical, mathematical truths. This bifurcation into a posteriori matter of fact and apriori relations of ideas is also known as Hume's fork. According to Hume, causation is neither given in the sense of impressions and neither a necessary relation. Causality requires us to transcend the evidence given in the sense of impressions. Such critique of causation which forms the informal ground for induction is a sub-problem within the famous problem of induction as given by Hume. We are mainly concerned about his critique of causation and the regularity view of causation that he holds.

There are seven different kinds of philosophical relations according to Hume. These are resemblance, identity, relations of time and place, proportion in quantity or number, degrees in any quality, contrariety and causation.

All kinds of reasoning consist in nothing but a comparison and a discovery of those relations, either constant or inconstant, which two objects or more bear to each other. (Hume 1896)

According to Hume this comparison can be done when both objects are present to the senses or one of them is present or neither of them is present. The relations of contrariety, resemblance and degrees of quality are not demonstrable but are rather intuitive ones. The relations of contrariety, resemblance, degrees of quality and resemblance are foundational to science. The relation of identity and situation in time and place are the only relations which are directly given in perception. While the relation of causality is not given in perception. While the other relations are given in perception.

Hume's causal analysis is divided into two phases the early critical and the latter constructive. In the early phase, Hume sceptically criticizes the concept of causation while in the later stage suggests the regularity view of causation. In the regularity view of causation, one causal event, which is temporally prior succeeds another event as an effect and this is confirmed through regular experience and constant conjunction. The relata of causation in this view are 'events' or the ontology of causation is that of events. Events given in sense-impression are unrelated and according to Hume, some relation is mysteriously established through our habits by our association of ideas as mentioned by above two factors of constant conjunction and an experience of regularity. So the Humean theory is called the regularity theory of causation or the one based on laws.

6.2.2 Non-Humean view of Causation

According to the non-Humean view, causation is a relation between objects, processes or entities in the world. It is not mysteriously established through habit and constant conjunction, but a real-world phenomenon. The nature of an entity is an intrinsic basis for rest or change. Besides the nature of oneself, entities have active potentialities which are the external basis of change and passive potentialities which are the internal basis of change.

Active causal power refers to the substance's capacity of doing something, while the passive causal power is defined as a *potential condition*. The passivity of a substance is realized when a subject undergoes a change and receives a *form*. (Giorgi and Andrea 2021)

For our concerns the potential powers are important as we talk about relational inherence where form is generated in the form of information. This transfer of information is considered as causal. We will be elaborating this in the section 6.4.5. When a change is not natural both active and passive basis are to be invoked in the explanation of that change. We claim that apomatic powers are passive potentialities as the intrinsic basis of change.

As against the Humean position that causation is an epistemological phenomenon imposed onto the real world, we have Cartwright and Pemberton (2013) who takes the position that causal powers are real. Powers are capacities of entities which allow them to interact with other entities in the world. The word power over here is not used in the scientific sense as in watt is the unit of power, but in a more common sensical way that objects exert influence, objects have certain capacities, and there are natural tendencies. Even though it is used in common sense parlance it is scientifically useful (Cartwright and Pemberton 2013)

The non-Humean notion of powers is gaining consensus over the regularity view of laws. The reason is that laws are realized only in ideal situations (Cartwright, Pemberton 2013). The correct way to understand laws would be 'laws + ceteris paribus clauses. Ceteris paribus means all other things being equal then the laws will hold. It will never be the case that everything else is equal, other conditions will keep changing according to context. Hence according to Cartwright laws lie to us and they are true only in laboratories, the world is dappled not exactly orderly or chaotic. On the other hand, powers are a very natural way of demonstrating why some phenomena are occurring. Causation is not a mysterious relation epistemically constructed but ontologically naturally given to us.

Powers ontology (Cartwright and Pemberton 2013) is a causation ontology that differs from the Humean ontology of unrelated events. Powers are universal/particular dispositions that are instantiated in substances/processes. There are several theories of causation, including regularity, probability raising, counterfactual, and constant conjunction, in which events serve as causal relata. In contrast to these theories, powers are thought to be constitutive of causation, whereas probability raising, regularity, covariance, and so on are only symptoms of causation (Mumford & Anjum 2011). One cannot question why electricity flows from higher potential to lower potential to reach equilibrium, or why air flows from high pressure to low pressure to reach equilibrium pressure, which is its natural disposition or very nature. These natural dispositions are exhibited by the properties of processes and entities. These dispositional properties are the abilities displayed by the processes and entities under consideration. Powers, for example, can remain dormant if they are not stimulated. As a result, power in manifestation and power in potentiality are distinct (Marmodoro 2017). Instead of discrete, unrelated events as causal relata, power ontology proposes mutual manifestation (Mumford 2017). Dispositions are always directed towards something, and intentionality is always directed as well. Substance powers and structural powers are the two types of powers. Things have substantial powers as a result of their sortal principles, whereas structural powers are a result of the constituents (Marmodoro 2017) that make up the substance.

The problem of the "causal power actuality principle"

Though necessary, the path of inquiry within the scientific methodological purview, specifically the reductionist framework, is insufficient. For example, the reductionist framework cannot explain biological phenomena such as evolution or life, as well as psychological phenomena such as consciousness, qualia, and the meaning of thoughts. This inadequacy was the starting point for Emergentism. The literature on emergence is replete with various forms of emergence (Fromm 2005). The problem of whether the emergent structure is autonomous or epiphenomenal arises with emergence, which leads to the problem of downward causation. If something acquires causal power after it has emerged, then does the causal power truly belong to the emerging entity?

Causal power actualityprinciple

> For an object X to exercise at time t the causal determinative powers it has in virtue of having property P; X must already possess P at t. When X is caused to acquire P at t, it does not already possess P at t and is not capable of exercising the causal/ determinative powers inherent in P. (Kim, 2010)

If the whole affects its parts, this violates the causal asymmetry principle, which states that the cause should come before the effect. The whole appears after its constituents and exerts causal influence over them. So, within an Emergentists framework, DC is threatened by the causal power actuality principle. According to reductionists, special sciences or minds have acquired causal power P at t, and thus causal powers exist only at the lower physical level. On the other hand, a similar issue is referred to as the "qua problem," depending on whether the effect occurs at a higher or lower physical level. The non-reductive physicalist argues for causal influence in higher-level capacity, whereas the reductive physicalist argues for causal influence in lower-level capacity mechanisms. This position regarding reductive physicalist viz. mind-brain identity theory is represented in the Mental Functioning Ontology (MFO). MFO is a framework to represent mental functioning within the broader framework that we have seen in 4.5 Basic Formal Ontology.

6.3 Unified ontology of mind-brain (mind-brain identity)

Frishkoff (2012) is responsible for significant work on the status of the mind within the framework of BFO. In 'Unified Ontology of Mind, Brain, and Behavior,' Frishkoff takes a position similar to

Smart and Place's mind-brain identity thesis. Mental processes like cognition, emotion etc. are identified with brain processes.

The mental representations are identified with neural representation. The neural representation is an Information Artifact Entity (IAE). Identity is a symmetrical relationship, which means that A and B are identical. When one is reduced to the other in reductive or eliminative identity, the reduced one is removed from the causal nexus. As a result, in reductive identity, where the mind is identified with physiological processes, the mind is removed from the causal nexus. By removing the mind, the concepts of mental causation and DC are jeopardized.

Our position is that mental representation is neural representation but given multiple realizability and polymentation, neural representation is sufficient but not necessary. Most importantly mind can be attributed only to a person as a whole and not to a 'part' of the person 'her brain' given mereological fallacy. The dependency relation in the unified ontology of mind-brain is characterized by 'is a' like mental representation is a neural representation. So unified ontology of mind-brain can be safely considered tantamount to mind-brain identity theory. We on the other hand claim that the mind-body dependency is characterized by relational inherence. We also claim (as does Frishkoff 2012) that the mind is an Information Content Entity (ICE), having the following four characteristics which make the mind partially autonomous.

6.4 Four-fold apriori analysis: Partial autonomy emerges

The four-fold analysis of function, unity, property, and information (FUPI) adds warrant and backing to the authors claim about the mind being a causally efficacious Apophenomena and not a substance but an information content entity. These analyses are not novel, but when combined, they make the claim coherent and pragmatically viable. There are sub-analyses within each of the four points among the fourfold that make the main point more robust. It is concluded that the mind, as an Apophenomena, possesses apomatic powers.

6.4.1 Functional analysis

To counter the claims of mind-brain identity theory, the concept of multiple realizability is frequently invoked. Apart from the paradigmatic example of multiple realisability of software on various hardware architectures, we can see multiple realizations in biological functions as well. One of the functions of blood, for example, is to provide oxygen. In humans, haemoglobin - an iron-rich protein - transports oxygen, whereas haemocyanin - a copper-rich protein - transports oxygen in octopuses. The element iron in haemoglobin, as is well known, gives blood its red colour, whereas octopus blood is blue. In the sense that we are within the natural realm and have an example, hemoglobin – haemocyanin serves as a very good example of functional multiple realizability. Although it is undeniably true that a physical basis is required in such functional processes, it is clear that the functional level does not necessarily type identical due to in principle multiple realizable arguments.

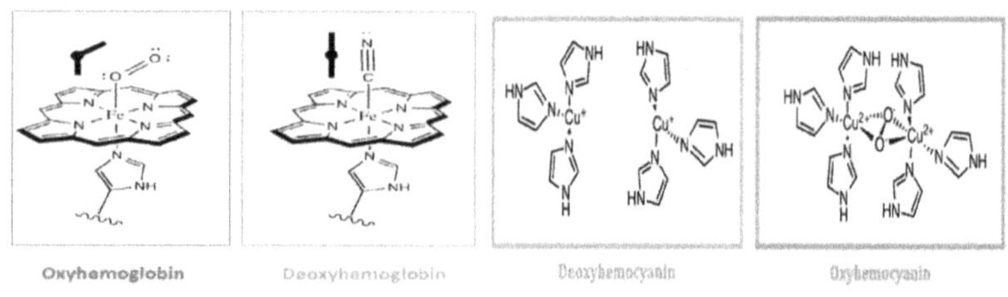

Figure 8 Oxygen transportation - multiple realizability hemoglobin and hemocyanin (images from creative commons licence)

In the image we have on the left-hand side molecule of oxyhemoglobin Fe (iron) at its centre, carrying oxygen and deoxyhemoglobin molecule which has transported oxygen. While on the right side we have an oxyhamocyanin molecule with Cu (copper) at its centre which is carrying oxygen and deoxyhemocyanin which has transported oxygen. The function of transportation of oxygen is done by two different molecules, which is an interesting case of functional multiple realizability.

6.4.2 Unity analysis

Showing a referent to a physically unified object is a simple task, but showing a referent to an abstract entity is more difficult. As previously stated, the mind is an abstract entity that is a generically dependent continuant inhering from the body; the mind can only be distinguished and cannot be separated. Because of physical monists' anti-substantial stance, the mind is identified with brain processes. Given functional analysis, it is clear that the mind is in principle multiply realizable. So, what is the mind, phenomenologically and semantically? We attempt to answer this question by drawing on the insights of various philosophers. Given the mereological fallacy, we contend that such psychological unity inheres (Patterson 2017) in the individual 'person' rather than the 'brain' (Boyles 2017). We have different types of unity. We believe that such unities are inhered in the person rather than being identical to the brain. We mention three types of unities hylomorphic, apperception and meta-cognitive. These unities are at an abstract level.

Hylomorphic unity: As we've seen in previous chapters, the Aristotelian concept of the formal cause is gaining traction in our understanding of DC. The hylomorphic unity is inextricably linked with form in the sense that *morph* means to form and *hyle* means matter. Kant's analysis of unity of apperception is because it is a necessary condition for the possibility of observing the phenomena. Meta-cognitive unity: The scientific name for humans is 'homo sapiens sapien,' with the word sapiens appearing twice and referring to the hominid who knows that it knows. Cognition is knowing and meta is second order knowing which is seen in the meta-cognitive unity.

6.4.3 Property Analysis

Because the book argues for a power's ontology in which properties and essences are important, it is necessary to examine properties. Second, philosophers who have traditionally argued for mental causation have relied on mental properties to make explanatory inferences. Cartesian dualism's conclusion that the mind is an independent substance, and the body is an independent substance is based on an examination of the properties of mind and body. The standard analysis is well known that the mind has the property of thinking 'res cogitans' and body have the property of 'res extensa' extension. From these two the dualism of mind and body is derived. The purpose of property analysis is twofold, the first is concerned with powers ontology of causation and the second is concerned with the causal powers of mind.

The Causal Theory of Properties (CTP) comes with two theses attached to it. CTP is the conjunction of two metaphysical theses: an essentialist thesis and individuation thesis. The former asserts that whatever causal relations a property enters into are essential to that property: if a property enters into a given causal relation in any possible world, the property enters into that causal relation in every possible world in which the property exists. The latter asserts that for any properties P and Q, P is identical to Q if and only if P and Q enter into all of the same causal relations. (Rupert 2008)

Property is essential in the sense that the property is a necessary characterizing feature of that bearer in all possible scenarios. While the second thesis which comes bundled is that a property individuates its bearers that if something has the same causal effects then they have the same properties. In the case of the mind, we are interested in its two properties firstly mind has intentionality and secondly it has the property of being an information entity. The property of intentionality is of prime importance as it is directed towards an object. Information in virtue of its form and structure acquires causal efficacy.

Properties do the causal work because what an entity is like depends on which properties characterise it and which causal relations an entity can enter into depends upon what it is like.........is a mental event causally relevant in the physical domain in virtue of mental properties that it involves or in virtue of physical properties that it involves? If it is the latter, and, hence, one denies mental properties causal efficacy in the physical domain, then one abandons any serious commitment to psychophysical causation. (Gibb 2017)

The qua problem in philosophy of mind question whether the causation is occurring due to mental qua mental or mental qua physical. If one accepts mental causation qua physical, then 'psychophysical causation' as stated above should be given up. One might still argue from the analysis of properties that even if properties are relevant in understanding causality this analysis ultimately leads to property dualism if not Cartesian dualism. We argue that it is misleading to say the analysis necessarily leads to property dualism. Rather than property dualism this position is best characterized as physical pluralism elaborated as against physical monism.

6.4.5 Information analysis

Given the information-theoretic formulation of the mind (Tononi 2004) and the higher-level (Ellis 2016), if one wants to conclude on the ontological status of the mind, whether it is reductively physical making DC same level causation or non-reductively physical which retains some form of hierarchy and thus makes sense of saying upward or downward, one must first settle on the ontological status of information, whether it is reductively physical or non-reductively physical. When we examine the ontological status of information, we can broadly divide it into three categories. According to Landeur (1991), information is physical. According to Alicki (2014), information is nonphysical.

But information is neither matter nor energy, though it needs matter to be embodied and available energy to be communicated. Information can be created and destroyed. The material universe creates it. The biological world creates it *and utilizes* it. Above all, human minds create, process, and preserve abstract information, the Sum of human knowledge that distinguishes humanity from all other biological species and that provides the extraordinary power humans have over our planet, for better or for worse. (Doyle 2021)

While Doyle, holds that information cannot be identified with matter or energy, it does require matter to embody itself and energy to be communicated ahead. If we consider the mind to be an information entity, we can generalize that mind with information properties should not be identified with matter or energy. determining non-identity with the material If we accept the analysis that the mind is an information entity, we are faced with the question of how the mind can exert causal influence. Collier (1999) proposes an information transfer theory of causation.

> P is a causal process in system S from time t0 to time t1 if some specific part of the form of S involved in stages of P is preserved from time t0 to time t1. (Collier 1999)

We have seen a return to the Aristotelian fourfold causation, namely formal cause and teleological cause, in the discussion of causation. Given the requirement of form preservation, one might think of this as a formal causation line of thought in Collier's analysis. The form transfer in this case is developed from the mark-transfer (Salmon 1994) theory of causation. This account fulfils the condition of causality for our purposes if we accept the mind as an information-content entity.

The causal powers viz. apomatic powers in the case of mind should transfer such informational form then we can accept the apomatic powers to be a valid account of causation. Another problem which is created even after we accept an information-theoretic view is regarding whether the syntactic view of information plays a causal role or semantic view of information.

The most dominant current view of cognition is the syntactic computational view, which bases cognitive processes on formal relations between thoughts. Whether or not the theory is true, it shows that psychologists are willing to take it for granted that form (viz., the syntax of representations) can be causal. Fodor (1968) argues that the physical embodiment of mental processes can vary widely if the syntactic relations among ideas are functionally the same. (Collier 1999)

According to the above quote, it is the dominant view that cognition is considered internal to the brain states is computational and the information is operation processed syntactically over the representations. As Fodor has argued that mental states can be multiply realizable i.e. physical embodiment can vary so the thoughts in that sense are not type-reducible. We do not argue for this, but subconscious processes likely occur by such syntactic processes. To measure information entrenched in such a form is to measure the complexity of that existing entity.

The quantification of form is a quantification of the complexity of a thing. Complexity has proven difficult to define. Different investigators, even in the same fields, use different notions. The Latin word means "to mutually entwine or pleat or weave together". In the clothing industry one fold (e.g. in a pleat) is a simplex, while multiple folds comprise a complex. The most fundamental type of complexity is informational complexity. It is fundamental in the sense that anything that is complex in any other way must also be informationally complex. (Collier 1999)

There are various definitions given as to what is information. Information is defined as a difference, measurement of order (negentropy) or complexity to quantify it. Here we measure complexity as information rather than informational complexity is fundamental to state that anything is complex. The concept of semantic information is far more applicable to the conscious psychological processes while syntactic information is best suitable for communicational purposes in the cases like internet data transfer etc.

Semantic information is a concept more readily applicable to psychological and other investigations than its communicational counterpart. (Carnap 1952)

Carnap has elaborately been discussed and is a pioneering figure in the semantic notion of information. That is the reason we consider that semantic information helps us understand our position regarding the mind/subject as the self which confers meaning to the world and itself. There are various ways in which we can further distinguish information viz. syntactic, pragmatic and semantic.

The syntactic information is specific in nature and can directly be produced through subject's sensing function while the pragmatic information is also specific in nature and can directly be produced through subject's experiencing. However, the semantic information is abstract in nature and thus cannot be produced via subject's sensing organs and experiencing directly. The semantic information can only be produced based on both syntactic and pragmatic information just produced already, that is, by mapping the joint of syntactic and pragmatic information into the semantic information space and then naming it. (Zhong 2020)

Zhong defines information as syntactic for a subject when it is produced by sense organs or through sensors. Information is pragmatic when it is produced by the subject's experience of the environment. Finally, information is semantic when the subject interprets, abstracts and synthesizes the syntactic and pragmatic information and confers a name to it. Thus, the mind is of the nature of semantic information and through semantic information, it gains apomatic powers and plays a causal role in this world. As it plays a causal role according to the Eleatic principle mind cannot be eliminated and is saved from being an epiphenomenon excluded from the explanatory process.

Our action, intentional behaviour is meaning oriented to achieve some goal (telos), or purpose, at times having practical needs rather than meaningless. One has to assign a name for information to become semantic so, language has to be in place and the possibility of coining new terms has to be in place. Through language itself, such tokens of semantic information can be transferred from one substrate to the other. The above fourfold analysis is various considerations to suggest that due to function, unity, property and information like the mind, the mind accrues causal powers. These considerations are apriori considerations about the nature of the mind. We also need aposteriori knowledge to base our claim upon. This aposteriori base is given by psychotherapy which by and large works, minimally to ascertain partial autonomy.

6.5 Pragmatic aposteriori analysis - psychotherapy

Psychotherapy is used to establish psychology's autonomy as a distinct science. Rather than asking, "Does psychology have law-like statements to establish its autonomy?" we ask, "Does psychotherapy work?" Beings with higher cognitive capacities, such as humans, have multiple degrees of freedom in that they can choose a path of behaviour based on their goals and desires, engage in counterfactual thinking, and even die in extreme cases such as war. At the metacognitive level, consciousness acquires semantic content and signals the neuronal level to produce a behavioural response in response to certain anticipations (Juarrero, 2010). The term "psychotherapy" refers to

> A form of treatment for problems of an emotional nature in which a trained person deliberately establishes a professional relationship with a patient with the objective of removing, modifying or retarding existing symptoms, mediating disturbed patterns of behaviour and promoting positive personality growth and development. (Wolberg 2013)

We have therapies in psychology such as Cognitive Behavioural Therapy (CBT), Rational Emotive Behavioural Therapy (REBT), Acceptance and Commitment Therapy (ACT), Dialectical Behaviour Therapy (DBT), and Mindfulness Based Stress Reduction (MBSR) that have empirically validated techniques for treating stress disorders, anxiety, depression, eating disorders, and cognitive distortions. How do psychotherapies work in contrast with pharmacotherapies?

Connectivity changes within these networks via "top-down (cortico-thalamic, cortico-limbic) or bottom-up (thalamo-cortical, limbic-cortical)" mechanisms have been proposed as mediators of treatment effects (Mayberg, 2003, p. 196; Goldapple et al., 2004). Antidepressant pharmacotherapies have been postulated to work via bottom-up mechanisms that target limbic or subcortical brain regions, while psychological therapies were postulated to work via top-down mechanisms that target higher-level cortical processing, such as cognitive control networks in cognitive behavioral therapies. (Weingarten and Timothy 2015)

We have both downward and upward causation and there is no inconsistency as is thought by the causal closure of the physical. These effective therapies demonstrate that psychological explanations and psychological variables are useful in healing individuals suffering from mental illnesses. From explanation to pragmatic application, this is sufficient evidence that psychology is an autonomous science

6.6 Generic identity

The Unified Ontology of Mind, Brain, and Behaviour does not include the BFO category of Generically Dependent Continuant (GDC). In Toulmin's model of argumentation, we present the claim that the mind is a GDC. The standard argument of multiple realizations demonstrated in the functional analysis serves as the foundation for this claim. The main issue here is the lack of transferability that GDC provides. The most common example of GDC is a digital pdf file that can be transferred and shared across multiple computers. In principle, we can expect such transferability and, at the very least, translatability in deep neural networks (DNN)

Visual cortical activity measured by functional magnetic resonance imaging (fMRI) can be decoded (translated) into the hierarchical features of a pre-trained deep neural network (DNN) for the same input image, providing a way to make use of the information from hierarchical visual features (Shen et.al 2019)

This transferability is a feature of the self/mind, which is formed through encounters with others. As the mind is an Information Content Entity, it acquires causal power (ICE).

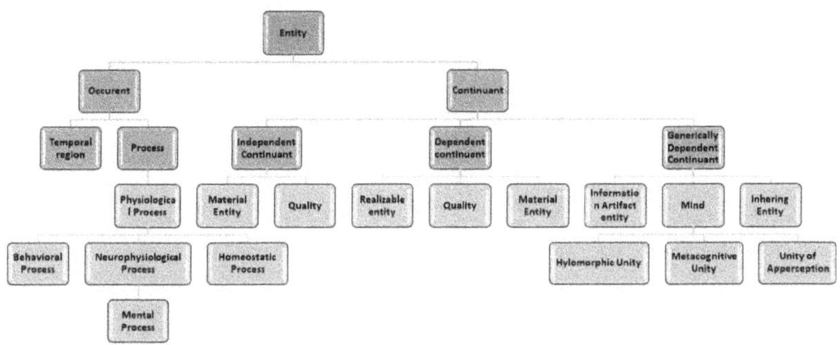

Figure 8 Mind as Generically Dependent Continuant

If the mind is an ICE, then the mind's causal powers can be very well established using the concept of causation as information transfer. This causal account via information transfer serves as the argument's qualifier. Finally, a rebuttal that there are other contenders in explaining minds' role in the causal nexus is a viable option. If multiple realizability is not true, the authors claim is jeopardized. Future work could explore the concept of neutral monism.

Individuals, units, and substances that do not have temporal parts are included in the classification of continuants. If the unity changes, the properties after the change are incompatible with the properties before the change. The properties are inherited in spatiotemporal components. In our language, continuations are usually nouns. For example, the red bus was standing there.

Occurents, on the other hand, are events, processes, or states that primarily have temporal components. When properties within occurents change, the properties at t1 are incompatible with the properties at t2. Because of accidental relationships between the spatial parts, the properties inhere in the temporal parts. In our language, occurrences are usually verbs. E.g. The 7:30 a.m. bus to the airport. Because of this primary dependence on temporal parts rather than spatial parts, the dependency relation of inherence is consistent with the functionalist argument of multiple realizability. We'll look at how these ties in with the concept of generically dependent entities later.

Given the analysis of property, information, function, and relation, a classification of powers based on the existents in Basic Formal Ontology is provided (BFO). According to Simons and Melia (2013), only occurents have causal powers because they are fundamental. The continuants only participate in the occurents' causal processes. For our purposes, enduring powers are causal powers of occurents, whereas enduring powers are causal powers of independent continuants.

We will be using this particular formulation to develop a classification of occurents viz. specifically dependent occurrent and generically dependent occurents. We can develop an alternative ontology if we change the presupposition of Basic Formal Ontology (BFO) from a substance-based ontology to a process-based ontology.

Rejecting micro-reduction and given the four-fold analysis we argue that only dependent continuants are reducible but generically dependent continuants have causal powers by information transfer and independent continuants have causal powers by substance causation. We are primarily interested in two categories of dependent continuants: a) specifically dependent continuants and b) generically dependent continuants. The mind is an information entity, whereas the brain is an information-bearing entity. The author argues that generically dependent continuants have causal powers.

Causal powers are argued to be granted to generically dependent continuants based on an examination of four characteristics: property, function, unity and information. If the fourfold analysis is correct then the mind is an information content entity which is a generically dependent continuant and in virtue of the properties, function, information and unity accrues apomatic causal powers of its own. Mind as a generically dependent continuant on the brain processes is viewed, which fulfils the criteria that emergent entity is dependent as well as autonomous from the lower-level given functional analysis and relational inherence. The mind is also an information content entity and as such can causally influence through information transfer without violating the principle of the causal closure of the physical given information analysis. So we can talk about downward causation and mental causation in a coherent way avoiding the causal exclusion by showing the causal efficacy and avoiding the causal closure by showing that inherence tolerates the mind as dependent and autonomous.

Independent Continuant

Independent continuants are the bearers of properties, qualities and dependent continuants. The standard exemplars of independent continuants are objects in our vicinity which are not dependent on others but are substratum for dependent properties like colour and shape. The relation between independent and dependent continuant according to BFO is given by inherence. Inherence is considered a one-sided dependency relation

Inherence is defined as a one-sided, existential dependence relation. This means that, in order for a dependent continuant to exist, some other independent continuant must exist to serve as its bearer. (Arp and Smith 2008)

We already have built up a nuanced notion of inherence in 4.3 chapter four. The inherence relation accepted by BFO is compatible with the concept of constitutional inherence stated in 4.3. This notion suffices when we have properties and qualities which can be categorized under specifically dependent continuants but not generically dependent continuants. The specifically dependent continuants are compositionally dependent on the relata. While generically dependent continuants are relationally dependent on the relata. In generically dependent continuants the relata can vary but the same role or function can be fulfilled even though the relata changes which gives it the features of irreducibility.

Continuant Causal Powers

Given the mereological fallacy, the concept of the mind cannot be attributed to a single part of the whole, namely the brain. As we saw in the introduction, abstract concepts such as humans are dependent continuants in the physiological processes that occur. Given the further examination of four features namely, properties, information, unity, and function, it is safe to conclude that DC is possible via continuant causal powers. The mind inheres in the person as a whole or the person is the bearer of the mind, the brain is not the bearer. So, the causal powers of the mental qua mental will be borne by the person as a whole.

In the framework chapter, we have seen the classification of existent entities done by Basic Formal Ontology (BFO) which is a domain neutral ontology. In 6.4 we saw Mental Functioning Ontology (MFO) which is a domain-specific ontological representation of mental processes. MFO is the unified ontology of mind-brain which is tantamount to the identity theory of mind we saw in 3.5 in reductionist physicalism. Concerning MFO we claimed that it does not take into account the further classification of dependent continuant into specifically dependent and generically dependent continuant. Now we elaborate upon the distinction for further clarification as to what is this classification not considered and how it makes our book coherent in the non-reductive physicalist tradition. This classification is developed to account for concepts like role, function and properties.

Generic Identity

Premise 1. Mental states inhere as Information Content Entity (ICE) in the bodily physiological processes given fourfold analysis.

Premise 2. Mental states are cognitive processes represented as Generically Dependent Continuant (GDC) in the physiological processes.

Conclusion: Mental states are partially autonomous, being generically dependent and causally efficacious qua information transfer.

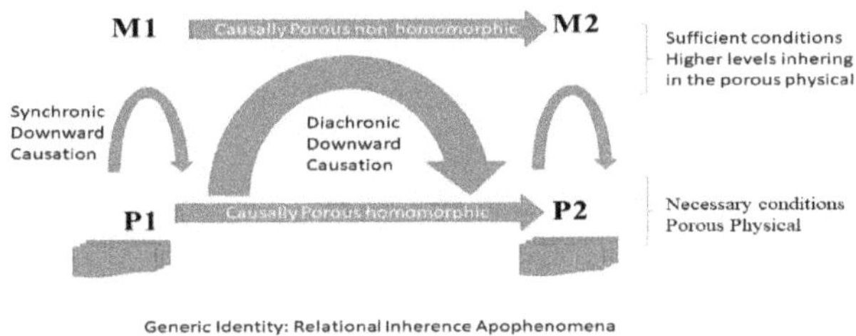

Figure 9 Generic Identity

Conditions for the possibility of Downward Causation

1) There be multiple levels to confer upward and downward causal relations.

2) Multiple realization and Polymentation for establishing some form of non-identity.

3) Relation, like inherence which can account for dependency as well as autonomy.

4) Rejection of micro-physicalism to account for causal slack at the fundamental level.

5) Higher-levels should be generically dependent giving rise to a new form where the form is in principle transferable.

When information is transferred from the lower-level to the higher-level in the formation of the higher-level it is called upward causation. When information is transferred from higher-level to the lower-level in the re-formation of the lower-level it is called downward causation. If the fourfold analyses are true and the dependency relation of inherence is correct then both the opposing characteristics of partial autonomy and dependency respectively are well explained by our position of mind as GDC (Generically Dependent Continuant). This phenomenon of simultaneous partial autonomy and dependency is called as Apophenomena. While the causal powers generated given the fourfold; function, unity, property and information analysis is called as apomatic powers. These powers are attributed to the person as a whole and not to the brain as a part. The mind inheres in the person as a whole and not the brain which is a part as seen from the earlier arguments of habeas cerebrum and mereological fallacy.

Physicalist Pluralism

We started with the debate between reductive physicalist on the one hand and the non-reductive physicalist on the other. The question to ask at this moment is what bearing our book has on this debate. The reductionist way of reducing and eliminating the mind from the causal nexus is problematic. At the same time the non-reductionist way of either epiphenomenalism or property analysis leading to parallelism or property dualism is respectively problematic. We have seen in detail about the problem of correlational dualism as parallelism. The book is inclined towards non-reductive physicalist position but at the same time holds generic identity which argues for a partial reductionist and a partial position of autonomy. So the best way to position in between Physical monist and non-reductive physicalist while inclined towards neither is a physical pluralist position. The physical pluralist rejects micro-physicalism where all causal powers are drained to the lowest level and accepts macro-physical causation where macro-physical entities have partial autonomy.

6.7 Conclusion

We presented a survey on how theories of causation are classified, such as Humean vs non-Humean, and so on. Then we discussed two relevant causation theories to support the powers ontology of causation while rejecting Humean events ontology of causation.

We conclude that causation in events ontology precludes events from being unrelated and that the condition of spatial contiguity is violated by Newton's gravity and temporal contiguity is violated by spooky action at a distance. We proceed from Aristotle's theory of causation to Aristotle's categories, and then we compare categories with Basic Formal Ontology (BFO). In terms of their causal profile, two broad categories of BFO are discussed. Simons claims that only occurents have causal powers; we argue that generically dependent continuants have causal powers as well.

In Unified Ontology of the Mind, Frishkoff takes a position similar to the identity theory regarding the mind. We argue that the Unified Ontology of the Mind ignores the classification of continuants as independent, dependent, and generically dependent. Finally, we assert that the mind is an Apophenomena, best described as a generically dependent continuant with the nature of an information content entity.

Rather than taking recourse to formal or teleological cause in the Aristotelian fourfold causation, if we accept powers ontology we can explain the phenomena of downward causation in terms of efficient causation. Apomatic powers are the efficient cause of our behaviour like how I raised my hand to answer a question in the classroom. Matter – hyle is considered as potentiality while morph – form is considered as actuality. Actual powers transferred as form as stated in the information analysis can very well fit in such an idea of efficient causation.

So, the mind is generically dependent as it is token identical and the mind is partially autonomous given function, unity, property and information (FUPI) analysis. Such an understanding allows us to capture both the dependent as well as autonomous nature of the mind and emergent phenomena.

CHAPTER SEVEN

Conclusion and Future work

The five problems of reductionism in the third chapter falsify the claim of mind-brain identity theory. The fourfold analysis provides a firm basis for the claim that special sciences and the mind have a real-world role to play in explanatory practices, and thus psychology has autonomy. As previously discussed, rather than pleading for autonomy based on special science laws, we base our autonomy on real-world application, i.e. pragmatic usage. So, in the simplest sense of folk psychology, we argue for the influence of beliefs in assisting our intentional actions. In a deep sense, we have psychotherapy and thus the claim of its autonomy based on apomatic powers endowed by the fact that the mind is an information content entity that is argued to be generically dependent continuant. The arguments can be presented in one place, concluding the traditional and contemporary views as questionable due to the fallacy of the contradictory premise and providing an argument in favour of our claim in a simplified manner.

To support the claim and respond to the problem statements posed at the beginning of the book, we proposed the relation of inherence as an alternative to the relation of supervenience, which was at the heart of the correlational dualism problem. The conditions for DC and the role of multiple realizations were presented in various contexts, but we saw it specifically and elaborately in the fourfold functional analysis. Third, the issue of higher-level causal influence was thoroughly discussed in the fifth chapter, which was entirely dedicated to the powers' ontology of causation.

7.1 Relevance and Significance

Downward Causation as a concept has its relevance in explaining emergence, free will, the autonomy of special sciences etc. If the concept of DC as viewed in our book is correct, then a way is paved towards understanding the above-mentioned phenomena coherently. This way of understanding DC also renders that the mind is not an epiphenomenon. So rather than explaining 'away' mind and consciousness, this way of understanding DC protects the explanatory role ascribed to intentions and mental states. We do not give up on dependency as we accept mind-brain identity in a generic manner which has benefits for instance in psychiatric treatments viz. psychosis using antipsychotics. At the same time, we preserve the psychological explanations for instance in psychological treatments viz. neurosis using Cognitive Behavioural Therapy (CBT) etc.

7.2 Novelty

The book contributes four novel concepts to the existing literature on the Philosophy of Mind. The first is relational inherence as against the concept of constitutional inherence which is the predominant meaning in the literature. Second is the concept of Apophenomena which is in clear contradistinction with the concept of epiphenomenal causation. Third is apomatic powers which are powers in virtue of being an Apophenomena. The fourth is the concept of polymentation which is the converse of multiple realizability. These are not new concepts but have some precursors in the existing literature. The book primarily crystalizes these concepts by coining words for these concepts.

Apart from these concepts, we have also raised some novel questions. One is that of reduction of Stenberg's theory of love in psychology to the molecule of love say oxytocin in biology, which we dubbed the 'hard problem of reduction'. The second problem raised in the legal domain for the identity theory is dubbed the 'habeas cerebrum'.

7.3 Limitations

There are primarily two limitations firstly if neutral monism is correct then mind-like phenomena become fundamental and not emergent phenomena. Neutral monism is neither inclined towards a physicalist nor idealist monism but regards that the basic constituent of the universe is rather neutral. If that is the case, then the question of whether that mind or consciousness arises later and can have a causal influence or not does not arise. The second limitation arises from the condition that there should be levels. If it is the case that there are no levels, then the question regarding upward or downward causation does not have any space in a flat ontology.

7.4 Future Research

Given limitations, future work will be directed towards process metaphysics. If we change the framework, then we get different categories and distinct natures of mind. In contrast to substance metaphysics, the metaphysical constituent is that of process. Rather than seeing two entities as opposed or as property or function (of a substance), process metaphysics sees them as a process (relational). The nature of a macrostructure is defined by its relations rather than its constituent elements, according to process philosophy. "It's being is constituted by its becoming" (Whitehead, 1929). Process philosophy (Bickhard 2011, Campbell 2015, Rescher 1996) is a different kind of philosophy than substance philosophy. Change, according to substance philosophy, is merely an appearance whose substratum is a substance (about which everything is predicated). Reality is assumed to be made up of static (essentialist) individuals, with dynamic features derived from the static individuals. The property still reigns supreme over relatedness for Descartes, but relatedness reigns supreme over quality in process metaphysics.

The future work also seems plausible towards the occurrent part in Basic Formal Ontology (BFO) which has mental processes as its constituent in Mental Functioning Ontology (MFO) given by the author. Can we consider mental states having causal powers in the occurrent classification of BFO, which seems to be a long-headed project?

7.5 Summary

In the first chapter, we introduced the concept of downward causation and stated the problems that motivate the author to pursue this concept further. Amongst the myriads of problems that downward causation faces we choose three major problems. The first problem is termed correlational dualism which originates because we accept the supervenience thesis. The problem of correlational dualism we stated is tantamount to the old problem of parallelism. While trying to escape the traditional Cartesian problem of interactionism which argues for two different substances, the supervenience thesis accepts only one physical substance. If we grant this presupposition that supervenience is the correct way of understanding the mind-body relation, then we land up into a world view where consciousness/mind is hanging outside the causal realm of the physical. The second problem examines whether we can have a dependency relation which can provide an alternative to supervenience. The problem is whether a causal powers ontology of causation can help us get out of the problem of downward causation. What role do causal powers play in the case of mind by which we can coherently talk about downward causation without contradicting the scientific image?

In the second chapter, we specifically pose two problems raised in the literature on downward causation which claim that DC is a misnomer. These two problems are viz. the relata of DC and that there is no consensus about causation in DC. We elaborate from the existing literature that there are discussions about causal relata as generic events, tropes and powers. While there is a growing consensus that Aristotelian fourfold causation should be revived to explain DC. We then pose the biggest threat to DC as the dependency relation as stated the problems of supervenience as a dependency relation.

In the third chapter, we begin by questioning the presuppositions of the Physicalist framework in which the problem of mental causation and DC arise. The physicalist thesis rests upon the epistemic virtue of parsimony which leads to a reductionist methodology. To understand further we discuss various forms of reductionism viz. constructivist, intertheoretical and mereological. We conclude in critiquing each of the positions constructivists are arguably resting on the foundations of observation when isolated observation is not possible. We raise a problem called the hard problem of reduction for the intertheoretical form of reduction. Thirdly mereological reduction does not abide by the six conditions of reducibility as shown by examples that in a cell which is at say the third level of biology is not only constituted by biomolecules but free radicals/ions are also playing a causal and constitutive role. The reductionist thesis culminates in the identity theory of mind. We pose five distinct problems which the identity theory would face if granted true. These problems range from the domains of biology, psychology, legality, logic and reductionist theory. The problems in biology are stated first as the gut-brain axis and the second problem is that of phantom limbs, which is suggestive that there is more to the mind than the brain states. The problem in psychology states that beliefs/placebo-induced pathways are disruptive pathways and have similar effects to that of medical pills composed of various chemicals. The next problem for mind-brain identity that we pose is from the legal domain. If the brain processes are where all the causal work is going on related to our behaviour, then we as persons are not responsible for our actions and legal vocabulary like the habeas corpus cannot be justified. We need at least one of these intentions, knowledge, negligence, and recklessness in the act/behaviour which are not attributed to the brain but the person as a whole. Then we discuss that brain is a sufficient condition but is it a necessary condition given the existing argument of multiple realizability. We give an empirical example of multiple realisability in analysing the idea of a functionalist viz. function of oxygen transportation in octopus done by haemocyanin vis-a-vis oxygen transportation done by hemoglobin in humans. We come up with a new concept which is the converse of multiple realizability i.e. polymentation. Polymentation is when we have multiple mental states like social pain or isolation realized by the same brain states by which physical pain is said to be realized. This makes the mind a process which is partially autonomous and through the relation of inherence dependent upon the bodily processes. It is not related to the brain, nervous system or the body by the relation of identity but by the relation of inherence. Next, we discuss the hard problem of reduction where we ask the question if we can reduce Stenberg's theory in psychology to the molecule of love oxytocin in biology.

In the fourth chapter, we discuss the framework suitable for our book. This consists of three major components. The first component is the dependency relation of Inherence which is claimed to be an alternative to the relation of supervenience because of which the problem of correlational dualism originates. The second is the framework of robust reduction an alternative to the standard reductive physicalist discussed in the third chapter. The third component is the framework of Basic Formal Ontology (BFO) which we use to represent the status of the mind as generically dependent continuant (GDC) in the sixth chapter.

In the fifth chapter, we discuss the second concern of DC viz. that it faces the problem of self-causation. This problem comes up because of the transitivity property of causation. If we question this assumption of transitivity in causal relations and accept a mutual manifestation of causal powers, then we can circumvent this problem of self-causation. For showing that the understanding of causation as mutual manifestation is correct, we have elaborated through two counterexamples in the literature. Specifically, we analysed the first example of the tree being dependent on its leaves and the leaves being dependent upon the tree. The example of two books standing against each other. We discuss how self-organizing systems can overcome the problem of self-causation by constraints interpretation of causation. Finally, we state enabling and disabling constraints and favour enabling as creating the possibility of lower-level whereas disabling constraints as higher-level selections and causal influence over the lower-level components.

In the final sixth chapter, we present our main argument and contribution to the existing literature on the Philosophy of mind. To set the context we discuss Humean and non-Humean positions regarding causation and how powers ontology argues for a realist position against the causal nominalism of Hume. Then we bring in the discussion of relata of causation in DC viz. powers and events. Relata in the case of reductive explanation are events. Events (not generic events) ontology by accepting supervenience precludes emergence, mental causation and downward causation. One such instance of identity reduction which we saw in the third chapter is the unified ontology of the mind-brain presented as Mental Functioning Ontology (MFO). MFO ignores a crucial distinction between specifically dependent continuant (SDC) and generically dependent continuant (GDC). We claim that the mind is a generically dependent continuant.

Then we face the question as to how causal powers arise in the case of the mind which is a generically dependent continuant. To answer this question, we analyse four concepts of function, unity, property and information. Through the analysis, we state that the mind is a partially autonomous generically dependent continuant. In virtue of being dependent as well as partially autonomous in the non-reductive physicalist, we coin the word Apophenomena for understanding the status of the mind as against the concept of epiphenomena. This grants what we call apomatic powers to the mind. This form of reasoning is apriori reasoning based on the fourfold analyses of function, unity, property and information (FUPI). To pragmatically support this claim, we qualify it by discussing psychotherapy as practically working on the mental disorders broadly labelled as neurosis. Rather than the traditional way of asking whether there are laws in psychology which could grant its autonomy in psychological explanation we think this pragmatic approach is more suitable.

We conclude our book by stating the significance and limitations of the book. The significance lies in the explanatory process that the book can explain both dependency and autonomy of the mind as generically dependent continuant. While the limitations are twofold, if the position of neutral monism is correct then the mind (panprotopsychist) is in some sense universally present, and it is not an emergent phenomenon. This makes downward causation redundant. Secondly, if we remove the condition that there are levels and accept a flat ontology then there is no upward- downward possible way of speaking. This again also makes the discussion of DC obsolete.

Future research might be taken in the direction of process philosophy as it takes the primacy of relations over relata. One more possible direction is regarding the mental states as having causal powers in virtue of being occurents rather than continuants, but this is a long-headed project in itself.

Works Cited

- Alexander, Samuel. *Space, time, and deity.* Vol. 2. Macmillan, (1920).
- Alicki, Robert. "Information is not physical." *arXiv preprint arXiv:1402.2414* (2014).
- Andersen, Peter Bøgh, et al. "Downward causation." Aarhus University Press (2000).
- Anjum, Rani Lill, and Stephen Mumford. "Emergence and demergence." *Philosophical and scientific perspectives on downward causation.* Routledge, (2017). 92-109.
- Aristotle, Jonathan Barnes. *The complete works of Aristotle.* Princeton, NJ: Princeton University Press, (1984).
- Arp, Robert, Barry Smith, and Andrew D. Spear. *Building ontologies with basic formal ontology.* Mit Press, (2015).
- Arshinov, Vladimir, and Christian Fuchs, eds. *Causality, emergence, self-organisation.* Moscow: NIA-Priroda, 2003.
- Assaturian, Sosseh. "What's Eleatic about the Eleatic Principle?" *Revista Archai* (2021).
- Bassett, Danielle S., and Michael S. Gazzaniga. "Understanding complexity in the human brain." *Trends in cognitive sciences* 15.5 (2011): 200-209.
- Bechtel, W., and R. C. Richardson. "Vitalism, [in:] E. Craig." (1998).
- Bedau, Mark A. "Is weak emergence just in the mind?" *Minds and Machines* 18.4 (2008): 443-459.
- Bedau, Mark. "Downward causation and the autonomy of weak emergence." *Principia: an international journal of epistemology* 6.1 (2002): 5-50.
- Ben-Menahem, Yemima. "From Causal Relations to Causal Constraints." (2018).
- Black, Max. "The identity of indiscernibles." *Mind* 61.242 (1952): 153-164.

- Bohm, David. *Causality and chance in modern physics.* Routledge, (2004).
- Boyles, Deron & Garrison, Jim. The Mind is not the Brain: John Dewey, Neuroscience, and Avoiding the Mereological Fallacy. Dewey Studies 1 (2017) (1):111-130
- Brooks, Daniel S. "In defense of levels: layer cakes and guilt by association." *Biological Theory* 12.3 (2017): 142-156.
- Bunge, Mario Augusto. "Causality the place of the causal principle in modern science." (1959).
- Campbell, Donald T. "'Downward causation'in hierarchically organised biological systems." *Studies in the Philosophy of Biology.* Palgrave, London, (1974). 179-186.
- Campbell, Richard. *The metaphysics of emergence.* Springer, 2015.
- Carnap, Rudolf, and Paul A. Schilpp. *The Philosophy of Rudolf Carnap.* Cambridge: Cambridge University Press, (1963).
- Carnap, Rudolf, and Yehoshua Bar-Hillel. "An outline of a theory of semantic information." (1952).
- Cartwright, Nancy, and John Pemberton. "Aristotelian powers: Without them, what would modern science do?" *Powers and Capacities in Philosophy.* Routledge, 2013. 93-112.
- Chalmers, David. "The hard problem of consciousness." *The Blackwell companion to consciousness* (2007): 225-235.
- Collier, John D. "Causation is the transfer of information." *Causation and laws of nature.* Springer, Dordrecht, 1999. 215-245.
- Coulter, Ian, Pamela Snider, and Amy Neil. "Vitalism–a worldview revisited: a critique of vitalism and its implications for integrative medicine." *Integrative Medicine: A Clinician's Journal* 18.3 (2019): 60.
- Crane, Tim. "Elements of Mind." Oxford University Press, (2001).
- Davidson, Donald. "Mental events." *Contemporary Materialism.* Routledge, (2002). 122-137.
- Doyle, R., 2021. *The Information Philosopher - dedicated to the*

new information philosophy. [online] Informationphilosopher.com. Available at: <https://www.informationphilosopher.com/> [Accessed 2 August 2021].

- Dewey, John. "The early works/1 1882-1888; Early essays and Leibniz's new essays concerning the human understanding." *The early works 1882-1898* (1988).
- Dronkers, N., and J. Baldo. *Encyclopedia of neuroscience.* Ed. Larry R. Squire. Vol. 2. Amsterdam, The Netherlands: Elsevier, (2009).
- Eisenberger, Naomi I. "The neural bases of social pain: evidence for shared representations with physical pain." *Psychosomatic medicine* 74.2 (2012): 126.
- Ellis, George FR, Denis Noble, and Timothy O'Connor. "Top-down causation: an integrating theme within and across the sciences?" *Interface Focus* 2.1 (2012): 1-3.
- Ellis, George FR. "Top-down causation and the human brain." *Downward causation and the neurobiology of free will.* Springer, Berlin, Heidelberg, (2009). 63-81.
- Ellis, George. "How can physics underlie the mind." *Top-Down Causation in the Human Context. Berlin and Heidelberg: Springer-Verlag* (2016).
- Fodor, Jerry A. "Special Sciences, or The Disunity of Science as a Working Hypothesis." *Volume I Readings in Philosophy of Psychology, Volume I.* Harvard University Press, (2013). 120-133.
- Fodor, Jerry. *In critical condition: Polemical essays on cognitive science and the philosophy of mind.* The MIT Press, 1998.
- Frishkoff, G. "Mental functioning is neural functioning: towards a unified ontology of mind, brain, and behavior." *Proceedings of the Workshop on Mental Functioning Ontologies at the International Conference on Biomedical Ontology (ICBO'12).* (2012).
- Fromm, Jochen. "Types and forms of emergence." *arXiv preprint nlin/0506028* (2005).
- Gibb, Sophie C. "The Mental Causation Debate and Qua

Problems." *Philosophical and Scientific Perspectives on Downward Causation.* Routledge, 2017. 265-277.

- Gill, Mary Louise. *Aristotle on substance: The paradox of unity.* Princeton University Press, (1989).
- Giorgi, Rodolfo, and Andrea Lavazza. "The self and its causal powers between metaphysics and science." *European Journal for Philosophy of Science* 11.1 (2021): 1-25
- Godfrey-Smith, Peter. "Causal pluralism." *The Oxford handbook of causation* (2009): 326-337.
- Green, Sara. "Scale dependency and downward causation in biology." *Philosophy of Science* 85.5 (2018): 998-1011.
- Hannikainen, Ivar. "Questioning the causal inheritance principle." *Theoria. Revista de Teoría, Historia y Fundamentos de la Ciencia* 25.3 (2010): 261-277.
- Hulswit, Menno. "How causal is downward causation?" *Journal for General Philosophy of Science* 36.2 (2005): 261-287.
- Hume, David. *A treatise of human nature.* Clarendon Press, (1896).
- Johnson, William Ernest. *Logic.* Cambridge University Press, (1921).
- Juarrero, Alicia. "Causality as constraint." *Evolutionary systems.* Springer, Dordrecht, 1998. 233-242.
- Juarrero, Alicia. "Downward Causation: Polanyi and Prigogine." *Tradition and Discovery: The Polanyi Society Periodical* 40.3 (2013): 4-15.
- Kilner, J. M. "Bias in a common EEG and MEG statistical analysis and how to avoid it." *Clinical Neurophysiology* 10.124 (2013): 2062-2063.
- Kim, Jaegwon. "Physicalism, or something near enough." *Physicalism, or Something Near Enough.* Princeton University Press, (2007).
- Kim, Jaegwon. "Supervenience, emergence, realization, reduction." *The Oxford handbook of metaphysics.* 2003.
- Kim, Jaegwon. *Essays in the Metaphysics of Mind.* Oxford University Press, (2010).

- Kim, Jaegwon. *Supervenience and mind: Selected philosophical essays.* Cambridge University Press, 1993.
- Kipling, Rudyard. "I keep six honest serving men." *Just so stories* (1902)
- Kulstad, Mark A. "Two interpretations of the pre-established harmony in the philosophy of Leibniz." *Synthese* (1993): 477-504.
- Kutach, Douglas. "Causation. Cambridge: Polity." (2014).
- Landauer, Rolf. "Information is physical." *Physics Today* 44.5 (1991): 23-29.
- Latané, Bibb. "The psychology of social impact." *American psychologist* 36.4 (1981): 343.
- Lewis, David, and Lewis Ma David. *Papers in Metaphysics and Epistemology: Volume 2.* Cambridge University Press, (1999).
- Lieberman, Matthew D., and William A. Cunningham. "Type I and Type II error concerns in fMRI research: re-balancing the scale." *Social cognitive and affective neuroscience* 4.4 (2009): 423-428.
- Lloyd, Morgan C. "Life, Mind, and Spirit: Emergent Evolution. Williams and Norgate, Ltd: London." (1925).
- Marmodoro, Anna. "Power mereology: structural powers versus substantial powers." *Philosophical and scientific perspectives on downward causation.* Routledge, (2017). 110-127.
- Marmodoro, Anna. *Aristotle on perceiving objects.* Oxford University Press, (2014).
- Mayr, Erasmus. "Powers and Downward Causation." *Philosophical and Scientific Perspectives on Downward Causation.* Routledge, 2017. 76-91.
- Mayo, Deborah G., and David Hand. "Statistical significance and its critics: practicing damaging science, or damaging scientific practice?" *Synthese* 200.3 (2022): 1-33.
- Mazzochi, F. "Complexity in biology." *EMBO Rep* 9 (2008): 10-14.
- McGivern, Patrick. "Levels of reality and scales of application." *Properties, Powers and Structures.* Routledge, 2013. 55-70.

- McLaughlin, Brian P. "British emergentism." *The Routledge handbook of emergence.* Routledge, (2019). 23-35.
- McLaughlin, Brian, and Karen Bennett. "Supervenience." *The Stanford Encyclopedia of Philosophy* (Summer 2021 Edition), Edward N. Zalta (ed.), URL = https://plato.stanford.edu/archives/sum2021/entries/supervenience/, (2005).
- Medawar, Peter. "Reduction and Emergence." *Studies in the philosophy of biology: Reduction and related problems* (1974): 57.
- Mellor, Tim and Crane D H. "There is no question of physicalism." *Contemporary materialism.* Routledge, (2002). 79-100.
- Moore, George Edward. "A defence of common sense." (1925): 32-59.
- Morowitz, Harold J. *The emergence of everything: How the world became complex.* Oxford University Press, USA, (2004).
- Mumford, Stephen, and Rani Lill Anjum. *Getting causes from powers.* Oxford University Press, (2011).
- Nagel, Ernest. "The logic of reduction in the sciences." *Erkenntnis* 5 (1935): 46-52.
- Nagel, Ernest. "The structure of science: Problems in the logic of scientific explanation." *Mind* 72.287 (1961).
- Negru, Teodor. "Self-organization and autonomy: Emergence of degrees of freedom in dynamical systems." *Filosofia Unisinos/ Unisinos Journal of Philosophy* 17.2 (2016): 121-131.
- Neurath, Otto. "Unified science and psychology." *Unified science.* Springer, Dordrecht, (1987). 1-23.
- Nicholls, Angus. "Review Symposium: The Fremdling of Teleology, or: On Roger Smith's Being Human: Roger Smith, Being Human: Historical Knowledge and the Creation of Human Nature. Manchester and New York: Manchester University Press, 2007. *History of the Human Sciences* 23.5 (2010): 194-201.
- O'Connor, Timothy, and Hong Yu Wong. "The metaphysics of emergence." *Noûs* 39.4 (2005): 658-678.
- Oppenheim, Paul, and Hilary Putnam. "Unity of science as a working hypothesis." (1958).

- Paoletti, Michele Paolini, and Francesco Orilia, eds. *Philosophical and scientific perspectives on downward causation*. New York: Routledge, (2017).
- Paoletti, Michele Paolini. "How I (freely) raised my arm. Downward, structural, substance causation." *Mind and Matter* 14.2 (2016): 203-208.
- Papineau, David. "The rise of physicalism." *Proper Ambition of Science*. Routledge, (2013). 182-216.
- Parfit, Derek. "Persons, bodies, and human beings." *Contemporary debates in metaphysics* (2008): 177-208.
- Patterson, Matthew. *Emergence and Causal Powers*. Diss. Durham University, 2017.
- Pinker, Steven. *How the mind works*. Vol. 524. Norton: New York, (1997).
- Place, Ullin T. "Materialism as a scientific hypothesis." *The Mind-Brain Identity Theory*. Palgrave, London, (1970). 83-86.
- Place, Ullin T. "Token-versus type-identity physicalism." *Anthropology and Philosophy* 3.2 (1999).
- Psillos, Stathis. "The inherence and directedness of powers." *Reconsidering Causal Powers: Historical and Conceptual Perspectives* (2021): 45-67.
- Putnam, Hilary. "Psychological predicates." *Art, mind, and religion* 1 (1967): 37-48.
- Quine, Willard van Orman. "Two dogmas of empiricism." *Can theories be refuted?* Springer, Dordrecht, (1976). 41-64.
- Ramberg, Peter J. "The death of vitalism and the birth of organic chemistry: Wohler's urea synthesis and the disciplinary identity of organic chemistry." *Ambix* 47.3 (2000): 170-195.
- Rescher, Nicholas. *Process metaphysics: An introduction to process philosophy*. Suny Press, 1996.
- Ross, W. D., et al. "The Works of Aristotle. Vol. I, Categoriae and De Interpretatione." *Journal of Philosophical Studies* 4.14 (1929).
- Rupert, Robert D. "The Causal Theory of Properties and the Causal Theory of Reference, or How to Name Properties and Why It Matters." *Philosophy and Phenomenological Research* 77.3

(2008): 579-612.

- Salmon, Wesley C. "Causality without counterfactuals." *Philosophy of Science* 61.2 (1994): 297-312.
- Scott, Alwyn C. *The nonlinear universe: chaos, emergence, life.* Springer Science & Business Media, (2007).
- Searle, John R. *The rediscovery of the mind.* MIT press, (1992).
- Searle, John. "Reductionism and the Irreducibility of Consciousness." *Emergence: Contemporary readings in philosophy and science* (2008): 69-80.
- Shen, Guohua, et al. "Deep image reconstruction from human brain activity." *PLoS computational biology* 15.1 (2019): e1006633.
- Shields, Christopher. "Aristotle's psychology." Stanford Encyclopaedia of Philosophy (2000).
- Silberstein, Michael. "Converging on emergence. Consciousness, causation and explanation." *Journal of Consciousness Studies* 8.9-10 (2001): 61-98.
- Simons, Peter and Melia, Joseph. "Continuants and occurrents" *Aristotelian Society Supplementary Volume.* Vol. 74. No. 1. The Aristotelian Society, (2000).
- Simons, Peter. "Fundamentality, and Freedom." *Mental Causation and Ontology* (2013): 233.
- Slowik, Edward. "Descartes and individual corporeal substance." *British Journal for the History of Philosophy* 9.1 (2001): 1-15.
- Smart, John Jamieson Carswell. "The mind/brain identity theory." (2000).
- Smit, Harry, and Peter Hacker. "Seven misconceptions about the mereological fallacy: A compilation for the perplexed." *Erkenntnis* 79.5 (2014): 1077-1097.
- Smith, Barry, and P. Grenon. "Basic formal ontology." *Draft. Downloadable at http://ontology. buffalo. edu/bfo* (2002).
- Sperry, Roger W. "Mind-brain interaction: Mentalism, yes; dualism, no." *Neuroscience* 5.2 (1980): 195-206.
- Stoljar, Daniel. *Physicalism.* Routledge, (2010).
- Tabaczek, Mariusz. "The Metaphysics of Downward Causation:

Rediscovering the Formal Cause"; *Zygon®* 48.2 (2013): 380-404.

- Thebolt, Gabriel Arthur. "Emergent wholes and the porosity of dynamic objects." (2013).
- Tian, Li, and Xuguo Zhou. "The soldiers in societies: defense, regulation, and evolution." *International Journal of Biological Sciences* 10.3 (2014): 296.
- Tononi, Giulio. "Consciousness as integrated information: a provisional manifesto." *The Biological Bulletin* 215.3 (2008): 216-242.
- Varela, Francisco J. "Patterns of life: Intertwining identity and cognition." *Brain and cognition* 34.1 (1997): 72-87.
- Vul, Edward, et al. "Voodoo correlations in social neuroscience." *Perspectives on psychological Science* 4.3 (2009): 274-290.
- Weingarten, Carol P., and Timothy J. Strauman. "Neuroimaging for psychotherapy research: current trends." *Psychotherapy Research* 25.2 (2015): 185-213.
- Whitehead, Alfred North. "Process and Reality: An Essay in Cosmology, Corrected Edition." *David Ray Griffin &* (1929).
- Wilson, Jessica. "Non-reductive realization and the powers-based subset strategy." *The Monist* 94.1 (2011): 121-154.
- Wimsatt, William C. "Reductionism and its heuristics: Making methodological reductionism honest." *Synthese* 151.3 (2006): 445-475.
- Wolberg, Lewis R. *Psychotherapy and the behavioral sciences: contributions of the biological, psychological, social and philosophic fields to psychotherapeutic theory and process.* Elsevier, 2013.
- Yablo, Stephen. "Mental causation." *The Philosophical Review* 101.2 (1992): 245-280.
- Zhong, Lei, et al. "Integrating semantic and structural information with graph convolutional network for controversy detection." *arXiv preprint arXiv:2005.07886* (2020).

Glossary

1. Apophenomena - The prefix 'apo' stands for detached, derived, and dependent, while phenomena refer to the object of awareness in experience. In contrast to causally inefficacious epiphenomena, Apophenomena is a detached and derived yet dependent object of experience that is causally efficacious due to partial autonomy. Words like an apology, apogee and other words with the prefix 'Apo' have similar meanings, so Apophenomena isn't a strange term.

2. Apomatic – The prefix 'apo' means derived, detached, dependent upon and Matos means thinking as in mathematics. This term is coined in contradistinction with the term automatic, as the term automatic has now colloquially acquired the meaning of involuntary, machine-like behaviour.

3. Automatic – 'Auto' means self and 'Matos' means thinking or animated. The word originally meant a person initiating an act of her own will. Later and now colloquially used as involuntary behaviour as in a machine.

4. Basic Formal Ontology (BFO) – This is a top-level ontology in which everything which exists can be categorized. This is developed by Barry Smith taking insights from W. E. Johnson.

5. Correlation - Correlation is a standard terminology used in statistics to describe how closely two variables move with each other. Here we are specifically concerned with the phrase neural correlates of consciousness (NCC). More specifically the stipulative definition of supervenience where supervenience is defined as no change in M (mental states) if there is no change in P (physical states).

6. Emergentists supervenience – Supervenience is a standard term in Philosophy used to describe the relationship between the physical base and emergent states. In the Emergentists case, it was used to mean a new form of 'relatedness'. Refer to

reductionist supervenience to contrast it with the current usage.

7. Hylomorphism – Hyle means matter and morph means form. Hylomorphism is a concept given by Aristotle which states that all objects are made up of both matter and form.

8. Identity – Identity is a symmetrical relation specifically in logic when we say the law of identity, it means A = A self-similarity. Identity has two forms synchronic at one single instant of time and diachronic across two-time instants t_1 and t_2.

9. Inherence – Inherence is a dependency relation of an attribute or property to its subject or substratum the bearer. The term 'relational inherence' is a term where the attribute or properties inheres in the relation between entities and not in the entities per se. E.g. clothness necessarily inheres in the thread, but the design is created due to the weaving of the thread in a specific way. The design is an accidental relation in principle which could be otherwise or plastic in the sense one can un-weave the threads and create a new design.

10. Physicalism – The idea has sprung out of materialism and developed by the logical positivists that everything is reducible to observational statements. Physicalism is the term used to represent unified physics in its broadest way as a structure of laws describing the links in space-time. This idea was concretized by Kim in Philosophy of mind as; if there is a cause it necessarily has to be a physical cause.

11. Placebo – When beliefs cause positive effects, even though there is generally vague medication taken.

12. Polymentation – The concept suggests that as there is an overlap in the brain processes which realize distinct mental states e.g. physical pain and social pain, multiple mental states can in principle be realized by the same brain states. The concept of polymentation is the inverse of the multiple realizability thesis. The general idea can be seen in biological concepts like polypotency / pluripotency or linguistics as polysemy. Please tolerate my ignorance of Greek the most general form of it can be stated by the term (πολυστιγμιαία) polystigmaia, a substratum

which can support multiple instantiations. People understanding Greek language can please correct the form of the word.

13. Reductionist supervenience – The idea that there is no change in the higher-level without any change in the lower-level. There are many kinds of supervenience weak, strong, global and their combinations.

14. Relata – The objects or entities related to each other by a relation.

15. Continuant – They are named so because continuants persist over time even though there is a change they keep back some of the properties and identity is intact. They exist as a whole in space

16. Occurrent – They are in constant change or flux - changing identity as it manifests over time i.e., they exist in space and time. They cannot be conceived to exist in non-temporal dimension.

17. Specifically Dependent Continuant (SDC) – It is dependent on some independent continuant and cannot exist without it e.g. quality.

18. Generically Dependent Continuant (GDC) – It is dependent on some (one or more than one) independent continuant but can also be instantiated or transferred to multiple independent continuants in process as substratum e.g. Portable Document Format (pdf file).

19. Independent Continuant – It does not depend on other for its existence on other independent continuants immediately e.g. material entity.

20. Dependent Continuant – It depends on other continuants and occurents for its existence. It is classified into Specifically Dependent Continuant and Generically Dependent Continuant.

21. Universal mechanism – Also called a clockwork mechanism, it assumes that the universe is made up of unrelated chunks and the workings are similar to the cogs and wheels in a clockwork.

22. Universals – They are mind-independent structures or abstractions (depending upon what position you take) which

serve as an explanation for the similarity between objects or entities.